Coming
TRUE

Coming
TRUE

Seeking Truth in Self Later in Life
William Brown, LPC

W B
C

Coming True
Seeking Truth in Self Later in Life
© 2022 by William Brown

ISBN 979-8-9867255-0-5 Print Edition
ISBN 979-8-9867255-1-2 Digital Edition
ISBN 979-8-9867255-2-9 Audio Edition

Library of Congress Control Number: 2022914660

William Brown has no responsibility for the persistence or accuracy of URLs for external or third-party Internet websites referred to in this publication and does not guarantee that any content on such websites is, or will remain, accurate or appropriate.

Designations used by companies to distinguish their products are often claimed as trademarks. All brand names and product names used in this book and on its cover are trade names, service marks, trademarks, and registered trademarks of their respective owners. The publishers and the book are not associated with any product or vendor mentioned in this book. None of the companies referenced within the book have endorsed the book.

Although the author has made every effort to ensure that the information in this book was correct at press time, the author does not assume and hereby disclaims any liability to any party for any loss, damage, or disruption caused by errors or omissions, whether such errors or omissions result from negligence, accident, or any other cause.

This book is not intended as a substitute for the medical advice of physicians or the legal advice of lawyers. The reader should consult a physician in matters relating to their health and particularly with respect to any symptoms that may require diagnosis or medical attention. The reader should consult a lawyer in matters relating to their legal protections and options.

Editor: Eric Muhr
Book Designer (Cover and Interior): George Stevens
Photo Credit: Scott Beck

WBCS Publishing
www.williambrowncounseling.com

First Edition
Printed in the United States of America

I am gay
Three small words
A declarative statement of fact
A declaration of independence
A private disclosure
A public exposure
Coming to terms
Coming out
Coming true

This book is dedicated to all the individuals and families, especially my own, who traveled this road with such bravery and taught me so much.

Table of Contents

Introduction:
WHERE DO I BEGIN?

I am married to someone I love. We have children we adore, and we built a life together that hums along with normal ups and downs. I have also come to realize a truth about myself that I have done everything I can think of to suppress and run away from. This secret that I've tried to banish to the recesses of my heart and mind will destroy everyone I love and the life we have if it is brought into the light of day. This secret may also destroy me from the inside out if I continue to hold it in. Deep down, I am overwhelmed with fear and cannot see any way out of this predicament.

How Common Is Coming Out Later in Life?

If this situation describes where you are at in life, you are not the first and will not be the last to find yourself in what seems to be a no-win situation. Statistics about the number of straight-identified people who are deeply in the closet about their true sexuality are very difficult for researchers to measure accurately. Being closeted and in a straight marriage or relationship is more common than most realize, and men and women all over the world and across all cultures deal with sexual identity issues every day. How and why people find themselves in such a struggle is complex and not quickly or easily explained. Some find comfort in at least knowing they are not alone in a situation that feels isolating and unique. The emotional and psychological toll of hiding their true sexual identity often becomes overwhelming for all involved. The consequences of maintaining the deception of self and others can have devastating outcomes. People are more courageous than they realize, however, and they have a bountiful ability to heal. Stepping into truth does not have to end in complete and utter destruction. This reality does not mean coming out is not hard or painful—it is both. There are ways to move into truth with grace, respect, and dignity for all, which can lead to a better, if not always easier, place in the end.

I am a licensed professional counselor in Atlanta, Georgia. I came out in 2008 after being married for eighteen years and having two children. At the time, it was difficult to find mental health professionals who had experience working with the unique nuances of someone coming out after identifying as straight for so long. I, fortunately, found a wonderful counselor who had also come out later. Along with this significant life change, I went to graduate school to pursue a degree in counseling. I had a great education with strong faculty and training opportunities. I discovered along the way that the phenomenon of coming out later in life lacked understanding and research in the field, so I combined my professional development with my personal experience to help charter these waters with others.

Who Benefits from This Book?

The general answer is anyone going through or supporting someone going through an identity transition related to sexuality. I started a therapy group called "Out Late" in 2012 to help people who were coming to acceptance of their sexual identity as gay or bisexual after having lived most of their adult life as straight. Most, but not all, married and had children along the way before reaching a point where they could no longer hide their truth from themselves and those they love. In the group's initial iteration, men and women participated together, as coming to terms with sexual identity is a common experience regardless of gender. As membership shifted over time, the group transitioned to men only. I found that change to be helpful to more deeply explore all the facets related to the coming-out process and its impact on identity. A colleague in Atlanta began a separate group specifically for women coming out later. Many of the issues explored in my writing apply to men or women working to understand their sexual identity. However, my language and examination of "being out" socially will apply more to men and most often to men who have been or are married to women.

The experience I draw from for this book has been wholly with cisgender men. If the word cisgender is new or confusing to you, not to worry. I will walk through definitions of many of the terms related to the LGBTQ+ experience in the "Important Definitions" section of this introduction (page 9). There are also themes and experiences that anyone coming out at any time may find beneficial to their process. It is important to acknowledge, however, that the bulk of my focus is with this singular population and their family systems.

What about a spouse who is straight and often shocked by such a revelation? Their experience is also complicated as they end up feeling like they have their own version of a "coming out" process related to being part of a mixed-orientation marriage that they never wanted or asked for. They need support and understanding from professionals and the people in their lives to process their own shift in identity and circumstances. I am in no way trying to ignore or diminish the impact their spouse's coming out has on them. Several resources exist to provide some answers and solace to a spouse's myriad questions, which can be found in the appendix. This book may or may not be helpful to spouses, depending on where they are at in their own journey, but it may provide some context to understanding what could have driven the decisions a gay spouse made. Finding connections with other straight spouses first is initially more ideal for healing.

This book can help other counselors, professionals, family, and friends who support people facing the truth about their sexual identity. Many people in a supportive familial or friendship role have limited understanding of how to have a conversation about their loved one's process, as they fear they will say the wrong thing and hurt rather than help. This book can provide some perspective about what a loved one is experiencing, which can be instructional in how to be most supportive. Additionally, professionals who work primarily with straight populations can use this book to understand some of the nuances related to coming out late from a clinical perspective. Hopefully, it can help those professionals also recognize when, despite their fervent support for the LGBTQ+ community, their lack of knowledge related to the lived experience of the gay community where they live can be a hindrance at best and damaging at worst to clients seeking guidance.

A few caveats as we move forward:

Some clients I worked with over the years first felt more comfortable identifying as bisexual, as it fit more closely with having been married or significantly attached to a woman. Through education and deeper self-exploration, some truly came to know themselves to be bisexual, while others more closely identified with being gay at their core. Attaching to the label of bisexuality was, for some, a bridge that felt less intimidating and more accurate from an outside perspective. After all, if one is capable of having pleasurable sexual experiences with multiple genders, wouldn't that be called bisexuality? Until a person has the lived experience of pursuing relationships fully with others, it is impossible to know what label best fits. That understanding can take time and evolution.

Bisexuality is a real and true identity that can get pushback from both the straight and non-straight communities. Unique and often challenging barriers and stigma exist when coming out as bisexual and incorporating that into life and relationships. A bisexual person may be in a different-gender relationship, which many perceive as straight with all the privilege that affords. They may be in a same-gender relationship, which some people on the outside want to describe as gay. They may pursue sexual and/or affectional experiences with all genders simultaneously, which some may see as fickle at best and selfish at worst. The pressure to "pick a side" can be immense and leads to an extra layer of internal dissonance when discovering self and choosing to live authentically. Once again, my writing here is centered on gay men coming out, but many of the drivers and pitfalls are applicable to any non-straight sexual identity.

It is also important to note that sexual identity and gender identity are two separate and distinct aspects of self. For example, my gender identity is male, and my sexual identity is gay. When I came out, I was moving to authenticity in my sexual identity, and my work has been with others doing the same. Transitions to authenticity related to gender are a separate area of expertise for which I am not qualified to write authoritatively. Once again, there are some parallels to any path of transitioning identity with self and others that may be useful, but I want to be clear that the exploration and understanding of gender and its fluidity will not be addressed directly on these pages. A list of resources for those examining their gender identity is included in the appendix.

Important Definitions

Some of the language and symbols related to coming out, while intended to be inclusive and inviting, often serve as obstacles for those trying to come to terms with their sexuality. Pride, rainbow flags, and "LGBTQ+" can feel like a call to some public organization or forced political beliefs that actually drive some deeper into the closet. It is not unusual for a client to say in a first visit that they have no intention of ever marching in a parade, though many often do for reasons they never expected.

In order to develop an understanding of the out-late phenomenon, we need to begin with some definitions of terms that may be new or confusing. These definitions are meant to simply give context, explanation, and a shared frame of reference. They are not some kind of required belief system that must be fully adopted. Some people may be familiar with many of these terms, but for others, there may be understandable confusion about a topic that they worked hard to avoid for a very long time. Some of these terms are also in a constant state of flux and expansion as people work to include the vast and varied lived experiences related to gender and sexual identity and expression. In my own work with clients, I first explain the definitions that I use to provide some framework. By no means are these meant to be the absolute and complete definitions that everyone working with the LGBTQ+ community would adhere to, but they help establish some parameters that I reference throughout my writing.

Let's begin first with the term sexual identity. Many use this term and the phrase sexual orientation interchangeably. Identity and orientation are describing the same concept; however, I choose the term identity over orientation because orientation can sometimes imply that re-orientation is possible, which I believe to be untrue. Sexual identity is simply an internal setting that indicates what and whom a person finds sexually and affectionally attractive, generally meaning whom I want to have sex with, cuddle, and share romance and intimacy. I define gay as an internal setting that says a person finds themselves primarily, but not necessarily exclusively, sexually and affectionally attracted to someone of the same gender. Someone who identifies as straight would find someone of a different gender almost exclusively attractive, specifically, men attracted to women and women attracted to men. Bisexuality involves feeling sexually and affectionately attracted to more than one gender. Sexuality can also be conceived as fluid and not necessarily a fixed point on a spectrum. There are terms such as pansexual that describe not assigning one's internal setting to any particular sexual or gender identity, which can be a freeing concept for some. Regardless of the preferred term a person may use, I believe their sexual identity is naturally written and encoded internally. What they do and how they pursue a relationship are all behavioral. It is also my belief that our sexual identity is something we are born with and not the result of external influences. Such a claim can be controversial in some arenas, which we explore in more depth when we examine various cultural and societal conflicts regarding sexual identity in chapter two.

Now, let's look at all the letters used in acronyms to describe sexual and gender variations. What ties these various identifiers together is that they refer to anyone whose sexuality, gender, or relationship style lies outside of the male-female, heterosexual paradigm. Every letter, however, represents an identity that is unique and has its own distinct experience. The most common and familiar acronym in recent history is LGBT, which stands for Lesbian, Gay, Bisexual, and Transgender. It sometimes has had a variation of GLBT, and over the years, it expanded to include other identities as well. The letters "GE" stand for gender expansive (those whose gender experience or expression is not captured by a binary male-female model). The letter Q was added to include "questioning" (those who are unsure of where they lie on any spectrum) and "queer" (anyone who does not identify with a binary or specific sex or gender identity). The term "queer" is often the most off-putting at first with clients I have seen. Despite the term being used inclusively for decades within the LGBTQ+ community, many initially perceive it as a unique form of insult on par with other derogatory terms to refer to gay people. Even some older activists who worked so hard and sacrificed so much to claim being gay or lesbian have expressed discomfort with being called queer. Ultimately, the term is designed to include all the variations in non-straight and non-cisgender identities.

Other letters one sees more commonly are "I" for intersex (those who are born with genitalia that cannot be described specifically as a penis or vagina), "A" for "asexual, aromantic, and agender" (denoting a person who feels little or no sexual attraction, little need for romantic connection, and/or no attachment to any gender definition), and the letter "P" for pansexual, pan/poly gender, or poly relationship system (pan and poly meaning all or many—such as attraction regardless of gender, identifying with multiple genders, or engaging in romantic relationships with multiple people in a system). Finally, a "+" symbol is often added to indicate inclusion and commitment to the evolution of understanding the many ways people experience their sexuality and gender. Put them all together, and you have LGBTGEQIAP+. That is a mouthful! Sometimes the mix of letters is humorously referred to as alphabet soup. In my writing and work, I use the acronym LGBTQ+ for the larger collection of sexual and gender variations. A reminder again that this explanation is merely informative and not meant to be a pool one must dive deeply into as they begin looking at themselves.

Although I am addressing most specifically the experience of men who are coming out as gay or bisexual later in life, it is also helpful to have some working knowledge related to gender, as it is often referenced in culture and readings on LGBTQ+ issues. Admittedly, this quick summary in itself is just the tip of the iceberg, but sometimes it is best to start with just the tip. Traditionally, gender was assigned as male or female at birth, determined by genitalia. Gender, however, is more than, and in many ways, outside of genitalia. When you close your eyes and picture yourself, do you see yourself as male or female, or maybe both or neither? If your gender assigned at birth seems accurate, that is commonly referred to as cisgender. If your gender identity is something different from what was assigned at birth, that is more generally referred to as transgender. If your gender identity is outside of the male/female binary, that is more generally referred to as nonbinary. We all choose to display our gender outwardly in ways that society identifies, which is our gender expression. For example, a high heel shoe culturally indicates femininity, even though it is just a shoe. In fact, high heels were first worn by men in the Persian cavalry of the tenth century to help them keep their shoes in their stirrups, and they have been worn by men for various reasons since that time. Wearing high heel shoes today more commonly expresses femininity regardless of one's body parts, which is an example of gender *expression*. Much like sexual identity, gender is more and more understood and expressed in fluid terms. Ultimately, gender is how we see ourselves, and sexuality is related to how we see and feel about others.

How to Use This Book

This book is a comprehensive look at the coming-out late process, from the first inklings about sexual identity to being fully out and living a new and authentic existence in every aspect of life. The first six chapters explore how and why this phenomenon happens and will likely be the best place to focus for those who are considering coming out and trying to understand how they got to such a place. These chapters should be the focus for anyone early in the process. The rest may be very helpful once a change is in motion but could be a bit overwhelming to examine too closely too soon. These early chapters may also be helpful to straight spouses who may want to gain some understanding about what went into the choices that their spouse made along the way.

For those who have started to come out, or were discovered or forced out, chapters seven through fourteen address the many steps involved in what I call "getting out." Here a person is working to change their circumstances in order to fully live as an out person, and it can take weeks, months, or even years to complete. Oftentimes, a person may want to jumpstart their life as an out person before they are actually free and available for that. They may separate from a spouse and want to start dating right away. Unless the rest of life has been unwound, getting too far on that path too quickly will often complicate the journey in practical and emotional ways.

Chapters fifteen through nineteen address what life is like as a fully out person. Issues of forming relationships, sexual activity and health, assimilating to the gay community and culture, and the risks along the way are examined in depth. Hopefully, this section can serve as a roadmap and plan once the "getting out" tasks have been achieved. The final four chapters are dedicated to what living an authentic and fulfilled life as an out person can be like.

My hope is that this book can serve as ongoing reference material for anyone coming out later in life. Some sections will have different impacts and understandings as new milestones are achieved. My other hope is that mental health professionals and others in the helping professions can use this book as a resource to better understand the nuances of coming out later, as well as the evolution that just takes time for those going through it.

Dear Me Letters

Six chapters spread throughout the book include "Dear Me" letters. Each of these was written by someone who came out later in life. I asked them to write a letter to the person they were before coming out, before everything changed. What would you want him to know as he faces this journey? Where are you today, and do you think it was worth it? I gave each writer free rein to communicate whatever they wanted about themselves and their journey. Each person's story is very different, and one person's outcome is not a guarantee for anyone else's. These letters do show, however, that no one is alone in having come out later. Sharing the trials and tribulations involved can hopefully bring meaning to the letter writers as their experience helps others along the way.

HOW AND WHY DOES COMING OUT LATER HAPPEN?

Chapter 1:
UNDERSTANDING DENIAL

For those who instinctively accept their sexual identity, a gay person choosing to pursue straight relationships may seem quite puzzling. How did you not really know? Why did it take so long to figure out you were gay? Why would you knowingly put a loved partner through what is sometimes years of believing you are straight, only to shatter their world in the end? For a casual observer, straight, gay, or anywhere in between, pursuing straight relationships while feeling same-sex attraction can seem like weakness and selfishness at best. Some may think these actions were some sinister plan from the beginning rooted in questionable character. For those attached to someone making this transition, the questions run more deeply as they try to make sense of what facing this reality means for them.

For spouses and partners, the questions are expansive:

➤ Was anything in our relationship ever true?

➤ Did I ever really know you?

➤ Did you ever really love me?

Many parents have similar questions, no matter when a person comes out, depending on their own beliefs about sexuality:

➤ Is same-sex attraction just a phase?

➤ What did I do to cause this confusion?

➤ Why couldn't you tell me the truth long ago?

Younger children often have worries about what a parent coming out will mean for them:

➤ Where will I live?

➤ Did I do something wrong?

➤ Is this change my fault?

Older and adult children often mirror the same questions their straight parent may have:

➤ Was anything real or true in our family?

➤ How can I trust you or myself?

I have yet to come across a client who intended to consciously and maliciously hide their sexuality by marrying a straight partner. In fact, I have seen instances where a person revealed their same-sex attractions to a future spouse who equally believed that questions about sexual identity would fade away as an issue in the future once they were married.

Understanding how and why coming out later happens requires dissecting the intersection of so many forces that leave a person unable to see, believe, or accept this aspect of themselves. Those forces are not uniform for every individual, but common themes of shame and deep self-loathing often drive the bus. Messages and beliefs from family, culture, and faith overtly and subtly communicate that being straight is the right and best way to be. The desire to fully and publicly love, share life, and create family, which is inherent in many people, has historically been available only in straight relationships. When internal and external forces conflict, people seek to find clarity and consistency in thought and living that will bring them peace, safety, and contentment. A narrative takes root that says living outside of heterosexual norms will lead to family conflict, discrimination, misery, and even eternal damnation. Subsequently, the road to seeking peace, safety, and contentment appears pretty narrow.

Is Denial Real?

In order to more fully understand why and how a person cannot see the truth about their sexual attractions, we must define and understand the concept of denial. One definition of denial in psychological terms is the refusal or unwillingness to accept something as reality. Another explanation is that denial is a defense mechanism in which confrontation with a personal problem or with reality is avoided by denying the existence of the problem or reality. In other words, denial is the inability to see and accept the truth. When a person engages in denial about any specific issue or behavior, they seek to only consider experiences and data that support the truth they want to see. "Yes, I have two DUIs, but the cops target bars at night to make money for the state and bolster their arrest numbers. Who hasn't driven after drinking sometimes? I'm just an unlucky driver who got caught. I do not have a drinking problem!" Anyone can find issues or moments in their lives where they were in denial over something. Let's say someone was an avid skier in their youth. After being off the slopes for decades, they think they will be back in the same shape they were years ago. Unfortunately, they come home with a broken limb or two. This person was likely in denial about the toll the time away and the aging body have taken.

Lying is different than denial since, in order to outright lie, a person has to see and know the truth. Such a statement can really rile up anyone who has been hurt by someone else's denial. It brings up thoughts of someone "making up excuses" and "avoiding accountability." Reactions like that are understandable, but for everyone to heal, it can be helpful to know that accepting someone's denial does not free them from consequences. If a person can only conceive of themselves as straight for a variety of reasons, seeking a straight relationship is not a lie to them. Building a straight relationship serves to confirm the reality that they so desperately want to be true. They can feel deep love and attachment for a straight partner and even express those feelings sexually, further proving that they are indeed straight. Once again, these pieces of data highlight what they want to see: their own straightness rather than gayness. Straight spouses sometimes also step into denial about their spouse being gay when they consider that they have shared a sexual history together. Many more ingredients can enhance and develop a person's denial about their sexual identity. We will take a look at just some of them.

Dangerous Stereotypes about Being Gay

An important component to supporting the inability to see oneself as gay lies in the dangerous and incredibly limited stereotype of what being gay means. I grew up in a small midwestern town in the 1970s and 1980s. The only images or portrayals I had of gay people were negative and foreign. Gay men were leading wild and out-of-control lives, effeminate in ways that I was taught were offensive and unmanly, hell-bound sinners, and forced to live in the shadows where they belong. I did not hear lengthy discussions or sermons about such a preposterous and incomplete definition, but the beliefs were clear as day to everyone. When I took that definition and compared it to myself and what I wanted in life, I was not like that at all, and therefore, I was not gay. Finding other boys sexually attractive was a horrible curse I needed to hide at all costs, but it did not make me gay! I wanted to get married and have a family. I believed in God and therefore believed what I was taught God thought about gay people. There was simply no way that I was "one of them." My experience is an example of what many young men grappled with as they tried to make sense of their world and their attractions. The inability to see myself as part of this fictionalized and demonized gay community played its part in my denial.

The 1980s and 1990s also saw the development and growth of the AIDS epidemic. Early on, AIDS was dubbed "The Gay Plague," and that name stuck deeply in the minds of young men who desperately wanted to not be gay. Not only was it difficult to see oneself as gay at the time, but it was also potentially deadly. There were, and unfortunately still are, those who believe that AIDS was God's punishment for homosexuality. It took years for the medical community to understand HIV, the virus that causes AIDS, and how it did not actually discriminate based on sexual identity. By the time a better understanding of the reality of HIV entered public discourse, the psychological damage had been done throughout our society. And for some young men, it added another very big wall around their denial.

My undergraduate years were spent in the Chicago area at Northwestern University as a theater major (not very shocking in retrospect). College was my first exposure to openly gay people after leaving my small town in Kansas. I met amazing people and got to see them and their lives. I felt attracted to some and fooled around with a couple of guys with some liquid courage on board. For the first time, I caught a glimpse into what the reality of being gay in the '80s was and would be like. I also had two beloved faculty members die of AIDS rather quickly. I carried a strong desire to marry and become a father, and I found some women very exciting and attractive. When an angel from heaven, the most amazing woman I have ever known, fell in love with me, I had all the data I needed to believe down to my bones that I was not gay. I was in deep denial about being gay, informed and cemented by some facts. What I wanted to be true was true in my own mind.

Internalized Homophobia

Another force upholding denial is internalized homophobia (IH). Once again, definitions can be helpful in understanding this force of denial. Homophobia itself is defined as the irrational fear of, aversion to, or discrimination against homosexuality or homosexuals. Internalized homophobia applies those same feelings toward the self. When our own minds have been taught and trained to believe the worst about being gay, thoughts and desires about the same sex are understandably infused with deep shame and embarrassment. And so, self-loathing is born—and sometimes an outward loathing of gay people. When a person feels same-sex attraction that taps into shame and fear, internalized anger and anger turned outward can result.

IH serves as a never-ending food supply for self-loathing for closeted people. It sows seeds in anxiety and depression, and it reinforces the belief that deep down, one is not worthy or lovable. In fact, a person is flawed, broken, and damaged if they feel same-sex attraction. Living with those feelings can lead to all kinds of negative coping mechanisms, such as substance abuse, eating disorders, professional and personal self-sabotage, anger management issues, and volatile relationships. Each of these destructive coping mechanisms simply reinforces the belief that IH establishes: you are less than and will always be less than.

While this internal dissonance can fuel many destructive behaviors, it also can instill a drive to succeed wherever possible. A closeted person may seek the most socially accepted status in order to distract attention from such an inner flaw, "Look over here: I have a great job, the perfect wife and family, a beautiful home and car, go to a great big church, which are all the things that are most valued and admired by society. Therefore, I am worthy, good, lovable, and not gay." At least, that is what it looks like from the outside, which buttresses the denial of feelings and thoughts that are too shameful to be real.

Race and Sexuality

Coming out later in life after having identified as straight is a complicated endeavor, to say the least. When coming out intersects with race in America, the complications magnify. I am a white man, and I am afforded a level of privilege based on those two facts. When I came out as gay, I lost some privilege in certain circles with certain people. All the while, however, if I do not disclose my sexuality, I am able to retain such privilege if I so choose. Being gay has been sometimes referred to as an invisible minority status because it can't be seen with a simple glance. I will never have the lived experience of being a race that faces subtle and overt discrimination in my home community based on the color of my skin. Since coming out, I experienced some moments and situations where I legitimately feared judgment and physical harm. I will never know, however, what it is like to live with that possibility at any moment in any given situation.

For people of color who do live with marginalization and discrimination every day because of their race, the fear of receiving more judgment from the majority culture and from their own community can make the hurdle even higher when choosing to come out. Add messages within the gay community that objectify, dehumanize, or discriminate against people of color, and a person can feel that coming out would result in complete isolation from acceptance in any community. Being anything other than straight and cisgender will make already racist systems and communities appear even more dangerous, creating huge roadblocks to living openly and authentically as a gay person of color. Needless to say, the layers involved in choosing to come out later in life for people of color are complex and may appear and feel deeply consequential. The pressure to remain closeted and maintain the illusion of being straight can be especially immense.

Chapter 2:
FORCES SHAPING DENIAL

To get a clearer picture of what leads a person to work so hard to escape a painful truth, we must examine the messages and experiences that form the foundation of denial. I often ask clients to look at a picture of themselves as a baby. Did that baby believe that being gay was a horrible, shameful flaw? Was that baby born already hating himself for feelings, wants, and desires that he wouldn't even be aware of for years to come? The answer is, of course, no, although that is the image of a gay baby and no different in appearance than any other baby. That baby had yet to even learn to walk and talk, much less have higher thoughts and feelings about himself. That baby would be taught many things through people and experiences that inform what he believes to be true and untrue, right and wrong, and natural and unnatural. Much of the information that informs what that baby will come to believe and feel about himself will come from family, culture, and religion, a trinity of its own that will be powerful for many years to come.

Family Expectations

We will begin by looking at family messaging. No one can paint with broad strokes about all families. We should also acknowledge that some of the messaging that might negatively impact a gay child came from a good and natural place, hoping for the best, happiest, and easiest life for a child. Boys start to be socialized from a very young age with expectations of being strong, great at or at least interested in sports, and liking "boy" things like trucks and roughhousing versus "girl" things like playing with dolls or coloring.

When my own children were very small, they enjoyed dressing up and putting on shows for us. My daughter had a collection of dance costumes with tutus she inherited from an older cousin. At times my son would put them on as part of their performance or in his own private playtime. The sight of him in those outfits struck a nerve of fear and shame deep inside me. I was filled with memories of being teased, bullied, and called a girl by classmates as a child, which felt like a terrible insult. While I did not say anything to tamp down his playtime fun, I feared he did not miss the look on my face. My intent as a father carrying around this internal struggle was to somehow protect him from the pain I had always felt. It took many more years for me to understand the flaws in my thinking.

Role expectations about gender and sexuality begin with family. Again, parents may be modeling what they know to be true for themselves and raising their son in that vein with no ill-intent at all. Is there anything more wholesome and all-American than a dad tossing a baseball back and forth with his son in the yard? Parents commonly raise their children with the belief that they are straight and will one day marry and have a family, and those expectations are subtly intertwined in their child-rearing. These parental expectations establish the need to come out at some point, and every gay person knows the pressure from those expectations very well.

Most gay people can look back at their lives and identify that they started to have some inkling that something was different about them beginning at age five or six when they started to socialize with other children more extensively. It is just an awareness that most other boys are reacting or interacting in certain ways that are simply not instinctual for them. Of course, a child does not have the ability to name what is happening internally, but the feeling of being different as a child is scary, and different often feels bad. As a boy, I once heard my father describe me as "a lover, not a fighter" to another adult. I was probably seven or eight years old. My father did not mean harm with those words, and I am sure he was trying to make sense of having a son that didn't seem to have the same interests he had when he was a boy. Those words, however, stung deeply, and I felt I was a disappointment and somehow failing at being a good son and a good boy. His statement became part of the narrative I internalized about feeling different. This narrative told me I better work extra hard to be a boy my dad could be proud of, which among many things, meant being straight. These types of subtle messages from parents are pervasive and build on each other over time. Telling parents that you are gay is still one of the hardest conversations people contemplate having, especially if that conversation takes forty or more years to have.

In some families, the messaging is more direct and frightening. Some parents react harshly to any sign that their son may be a "sissy" or worse. Family communication that states clearly, "No son of mine is going be a fag," pushes a child even deeper into the closet. A person I know had a father who caught him looking at a bisexual porn video he got ahold of at a video store when he was a teenager. His father beat him to the point he had to stay at home until the bruises on his face healed. As this event spread through their small community, many believed the father did what he had to do when faced with such a horror, and the real blame was with his son. Many people today are lulled into a belief that such extremes are no longer part of our society. With all the visibility and positive role models, children today must be free from such heavy and fearful family pressure, right? On the contrary, kids are still kicked out of their homes and banished by parents for being gay. Families still turn their backs emotionally and financially on teenagers for simply being who they are. Researchers at the University of Chicago estimated in 2017 that forty percent of homeless youth identify within the LGBTQ+ community. The message taken from these real stories is that the cost of being gay could be losing the love and security of family.

In addition to messages received from other family members, many people have an internal desire to build and create a family of their own. Many carry an innate drive to connect romantically and intimately with another person, and those connections have been codified in the institution of marriage for many years. Historically, marriage was not based on falling in love with your soulmate and making a mutual lifelong commitment—far from it. A coupling of choice based on love, compatibility, and commitment is a relatively new concept in human history and a natural evolution of marriage to reflect a more authentic and mutually respectful design. For many centuries, women were considered property, and marriages were typically financial arrangements and agreements between families.

Arranged marriages still happen in various cultures around the globe. Regardless of its history and evolution, the institution of marriage has been a cornerstone of many societies for building community and families. Laws are written today to support the choice of marriage with many benefits uniquely offered through the marriage contract, and they are often critical in protecting the rights of both parents and children when they become part of the family structure.

For many years in modern western society, girls were socialized to imagine their dream wedding to their Prince Charming, and boys were taught to work hard and be successful to provide a good life for their one-day wife and children. While those sentiments might seem properly antiquated in today's world, marriage and family remain a gold standard that many use to measure success and stability in life. Given the combination of a person's innate drive to couple and perhaps procreate and society's gold standard norm for a happy life, it is no small wonder that seeking and wanting to build a life with someone and raise a family are still common, natural, and positive drives for many people.

We live in a time in the United States and many countries around the world where two people can legally marry regardless of gender, at least as of this writing. Take just a minute to let that statement sink in. Marriage between two people of the same gender was absolutely unheard of, condemned, and vilified for all of time up until the past twenty years or so. There are many loud and prominent voices that herald that gay people marrying is a sign of the end times and symbolic of the complete disintegration of society.

In the United States, the Supreme Court is still working through challenges over wedding cakes, photography, and who "has" to host weddings between gay people. With the ruling overturning Roe v Wade in June of 2022, some feel nervous that the right to marriage for non-heterosexual individuals faces new possible risks in America. Society has come a long way toward acceptance, but there is still a long way to go before gay people feel the same access to community support and recognition that straight couples have and always will have. Today in some states and countries, gay-identified people are also legally allowed to adopt children or seek parenting through medically assisted means. That right is ever-changing and ever under threat, so parenting remains certainly far from a guarantee for gay individuals and couples.

Jump back before the monumental shift in some rights for gay people regarding marriage and family, which again is not a very far jump. The world looked pretty bleak for a gay person who just wanted to have love, marriage, and family as a natural part of their lives. Being gay meant marriage and family were not an option. Period. So, when a person was looking at their natural sexual attraction and their natural desire to create a relationship and family, the only path to the latter was to be straight or at least live life as a straight person. Some people fearful about their true sexual identity chose to pursue their natural desire for family by the only means available and the only means that their world gave them: be straight.

Cultural Messages

Popular culture is exactly that: popular, well-known, and reflective of its time. In order to fully understand cultural influences on coming out late, we must understand cultural history. Applying today's standards in popular culture to measure the safety and promise one may have felt about coming out at a previous time would be an unfair mistake. Today, one does not have to look very far to find openly gay people succeeding and being celebrated in nearly every industry across the globe. Gay artists of all types openly depict their lived experiences in the world, gay athletes compete at the highest levels, and a gay man ran a legitimate campaign for president of the United States. Messages of "It Gets Better" and "Born This Way" are readily available, and Pride-themed merchandise explodes across marketplaces in June to celebrate Pride month. We have come a long way, but just not all the way.

Imagine, if you will, which shouldn't be that hard (it wasn't that long ago), a world where there were literally no explicit references to being gay in popular culture. If there was an essence or tangential reference, the portrayal was always negative or glossed over. My parents used to love to watch Liberace on TV. They thought he was a magnificent musician and showman. They were right about that, but no one ever mentioned to me that he was obviously gay. Paul Lynde was a star in the center square of Hollywood Squares, a TV gameshow that ran in the 1970s. He made joke after joke full of innuendo about being gay, but he could absolutely not publicly acknowledge in any way that he actually was gay. The first character I saw on TV that stated he was gay was played by Billy Crystal on the TV series "Soap." He was wacky and funny and carried a ventriloquist dummy to speak for himself at times. He had no storylines related to himself as a total person, but he did serve as the butt of homophobic jokes. Every movie, song, show, book, magazine article, and news story was written for and exclusively about straight people. When I was a kid in the 1970s, rumors spread between kids my age about Rod Stewart, a successful rock star, having sperm pumped from his stomach. Such an idea was the most horrifying and terrifying thing imaginable, but people believed it and used it to vilify anything to do with being gay.

Needless to say, popular culture pretended like being gay didn't even exist, and if it did, it should be ridiculed and belittled.

With the onset of the AIDS epidemic that we explored earlier, popular culture could no longer ignore the existence of gay men in our world. Liberal-leaning types became very supportive and dramatized the horror of this scourge. Religiously conservative-leaning types used the epidemic to amplify the stories of fear and condemnation related to being gay. Movies, plays, and books written by actual gay people about their experiences began to be produced to popular and critical success. Eventually, more and more accessible and complete characters and people began to gain hold in popular culture, and advances were made along the road to acceptance. By the time culture began to evolve, many closeted gay men already had married and had families. A world that had always been unwelcoming to gay people suddenly became more open and accepting. The idea that a man could love, marry, and build a family with another man became something achievable, although costly and hard.

On a bit of a tangent, I want to explore some of the realities we walk through in today's more open and affirming society. As more socially liberal people began to champion the rights of gay people, they called out discrimination and hate. Even with these important efforts, a subtle but measurable hierarchy remains in which straight is empowered, and gay is not. Straight allies offer acceptance, friendship, and welcome to their "gay brothers and sisters." Statements like "I accept you for who you are" or "I have no issues with gay people" are well-meaning for sure. As a gay man, I am grateful to know where someone stands regarding my sexuality. Acceptance and affirmation, however, are still things granted by straight people to gay people. I wonder how it would be received if I told my straight friends that

I accept and affirm their sexual identity. I may not understand it, but I welcome it in the world! I hope for the day when we no longer have to speak about accepting our differences; we just do it as a matter of course. In any ally relationship with a marginalized community, perhaps focus should be directed toward those who hold judgment and actively display hate and ignorance. I would ask a straight person who kindly wants to let me know how much they accept me to instead call out other straight people who reject gay people. And off the soap box I go.

Religious Rules

Religious influences that support a person's denial about their sexuality have never been hard to find, and they continue to have the most visible and broad platform against homosexuality in our world. All major religions have a history of casting same-sex attraction and same-sex relationships as sinful and against God's plan and design. Religious teachings and religious texts are used to justify this belief, and many people with good intentions and good hearts hold to what they have been taught these sacred texts tell them about being gay. Many readily accept these teachings because such tenets simply do not affect them if they are straight, so the consequences of such teachings have no direct impact. It is often not until someone they love shares how they have been directly harmed by such teachings that many begin to consider the validity and impact of their beliefs.

There are also those who do not have good intentions and who use these texts to spread hate, discrimination, physical threats, and even death. Theology across religious beliefs ebbs and flows on all sorts of issues, and understanding religious texts within their historical, cultural, and social context versus the context of our understanding today is a continually evolving process. Many religious leaders, theological experts, philosophers, and regular old folks have written extensively on challenging the historical religious teachings regarding same-sex attraction and same-sex relationships in our world today. I am not steeped deeply enough in the research or the scholarship to write authoritatively on these issues. Resources that explore a modern understanding of religious texts about sexuality can be found in the appendix. I will instead focus on the impacts historical religious teachings have had on many men's determination to continue in denial.

When a young person is taught that attraction between two people of the same sex is unnatural, immoral, evil, and in some instances, illegal, you better believe they will think twice before acknowledging the truth about their sexuality to themselves, much less anyone else. When they are also taught that acting on those attractions will lead to family and cultural ostracization and eternal damnation, you better believe they will think three, four, or a hundred times before stepping into themselves fully. When a young person reads stories of people caught engaging in same-sex relationships being jailed, beaten, thrown out on the street, or murdered, all in the name of religion, I think one can start to understand how that person would want to run as far away from these feelings as they can.

What is a person of faith to do if they have these feelings and desires that are so fraught with peril? The religious response commonly has been prescriptive: pray harder for it to be taken away and pursue marriage between a man and a woman. With enough faith and obedience to God, these feelings will be washed away and replaced by the sacred love between a man and a woman in marriage. Pray it away! One observation I would make is that millions of people for thousands of years have been earnestly and fervently praying for God to take their same-sex attractions away. Perhaps God's answer to such prayers is, "No, variations in sexual identity are part of my design." That may seem simple and easy, but sometimes things are simpler than they appear.

My work has mostly been with those who have a Christian background, although the shame and guilt induced by religion are common across faith traditions. Many faiths, depending on sect or denomination, still encourage parents and family to reject and cast out family members who accept themselves as gay, and many follow through with that call. Once again, LGBTQ+ youth represent forty percent of homeless youth in the United States. Some in religious communities have adopted the adage, "Love the sinner, but hate the sin." In this messaging, being gay might be okay, but doing gay is certainly not. The prescription then is to commit to a life of celibacy or attempt to engage in a heterosexual marriage and sexual relationship with the goal of having children.

Regardless of the exact shape of these messages, the meaning taught is that, in order to be faithful, one must reject this aspect of who they are, period. In order to address the fact that many people of faith experience these feelings, religious groups developed various approaches to "fix" this sinful state of being. For many years, conversion therapy was practiced in order to snuff out same-sex attractions. This approach is based on the belief that same-sex attraction can be "cured" through various therapeutic approaches. Conversion therapy became well-funded and populated by religions and people of faith. The idea was that through negative and, at times, physically torturous reinforcement, same-sex attraction could be eliminated or diminished. The proposition was that success hinged on the veracity of a person's faith, so when it didn't work, it was due to spiritual weakness.

When conversion therapy failed (as it always did and does), it was not perceived as a failure of the therapy but instead as the failure of personal faith. Additional support groups for gay men began to develop through religious movements with the belief that if Christian men could be honest and hold each other accountable, they would be able to perform their duties as men and husbands in their homes. As for conversion therapy, it has been discredited by all mental health organizations and deemed dangerous and harmful. Many of the very large organizations dedicated to this practice, such as Exodus International, have imploded with their own leaders rejecting conversion therapy and often openly coming out as gay. And as for the support groups that still exist today, many men I work with report that these groups simply act as a way for closeted gay men to connect physically and emotionally under the guise of religious support.

Some therapists who are deeply religious in any faith tradition today approach treating people with same-sex attraction and religious angst using a twelve-step model of addiction recovery. This intervention is the new conversion therapy. In a recovery model, the behaviors related to same-sex attraction are considered a sexual addiction, and through the use of the twelve steps, that behavior can be eliminated, and sexual sobriety will ensue. The problem with this latest model of religious-based "treatment" is that it still identifies sexual attraction and behaviors as the problem. Some argue that if a person's same-sex attraction is causing them distress in the form of anxiety and depression, wouldn't offering them a sober plan be helpful? Such an approach ignores that the faulty religious teachings themselves may be the cause of a person's distress. Instead of looking in the mirror and holding themselves accountable for the damage they do, these practitioners instead want to tell gay people that they are flawed, unholy, and less than.

I want to acknowledge that there are many religious faiths, leaders, and communities that support, welcome, and affirm the experience and lives of gay people. Having faith and being gay can coexist fully. Many religious teachings about the sanctity of marriage, about being a loving and kind partner and parent, and about being a servant to those in need in our world have nothing to do with being gay and everything to do with being a good person trying to make the right decisions on a day to day basis. Whether a marriage is centered on a bond between a man and a woman, two women, or two men who love each other deeply and make a commitment to each other and a God they worship, that family deserves equality, honor, and a place at the table, pew, and altar.

When messages from family, culture, and faith align, powerful forces develop. Such forces can be for good and call people to lives of service, kindness, and love for one another. Those forces, however, can also lead to isolation, shame, and desperation when focused on judgment about sexual identity. When someone hears a consistent message in all three arenas that who they are is wrong, unnatural, and an abomination, and what they feel is a destroyer of peace, security, and salvation, then the foundation for a fortressed denial is often unavoidable.

Chapter 3:
IT IS WORTH IT

O ur first "Dear Me" letter was written by a man who started to publicly come out and change his circumstances when he was in his late forties after being married for more than twenty years and fathering two children. Throughout his youth, he struggled with his natural attractions and what they would mean. He sought help through faith to manage what seemed so dangerous and broken back then. Today he feels few regrets for his past and deep gratitude for all that has come to fruition since coming out.

Dear Me,

While I in no way can complain about how my life has turned out (in fact, I never dreamed it could be so good), there are certainly a few things I wish I had known. At the same time, choices made have borne so many blessings, making it hard to discern the path I should have taken. I cannot change the past, but I can learn from it.

As an adolescent with raging hormones, I knew my preferences. Gay porn hidden in my room (inside Christian rock albums, no less) and a penchant for fashion and design should have been enough to raise my awareness, at least today but not in 1985. The pressure was immense. Not only was I told that being gay was an abomination before God, but in a small town, bullying was real. The AIDS crisis was blasting onto the front page of the local paper, and loving a man was a sure path to the "gay cancer" with an accompanying first-class ticket to hell, not to mention the disapproval of my parents, friends, church, and entire support system.

Efforts to fix my problem led me to double down with conversion therapy, efforts to be more devout, and an unsustainable work ethic. How I wish I had known that what had been told was an aberration was actually a wonderful manifestation of God's love for me—exactly as I was created.

I will never regret having two beautiful children and a rich life, but I do regret the pain caused as their seemingly perfect family split up. As I wrestled with this decision for years, dragging a then supportive spouse through the ups and downs of false hope I could be "fixed," I wish I had known that pulling the band-aid off is often the more merciful path. I also wish I had listened to those who assured me that children are resilient—they truly are. And I should have listened to myself along the way. When I found love, I knew it in my bones but then fought to suppress and deny it.

Life does get better, and living authentically has so much upside—more real friendships, the ability to relax and truly enjoy life, a sense of peace deep in my soul, and the experience of genuine love. While this has come at a cost, it is worth it. So many of the worst-case scenarios did not happen, and while grateful for the journey, I can only hope that lessons learned along the way make me wiser going forward.

Chapter 4:
FAULTY BELIEFS

Another factor that plays into a person's struggle to consciously reconcile their sexual attractions and desires with their sexual identity is what I term "faulty beliefs." Many of these assertions are supported by those who hold the view that homosexuality is unnatural or worse. If you Google all of these "faulty beliefs," you can find a never-ending supply of arguments that purport to be facts. Some are openly taught in family, cultural, and religious settings as absolute truths. When raised with these "facts," a person has a hard time moving past such teachings when trying to make sense of their inner and outer worlds.

Being Gay Is Not a Choice

The first "faulty belief" is that being gay is a choice. One common question against this teaching is, "Why would anyone choose to be gay?" Given all of the historical and ongoing discrimination against all sexual minorities, it makes little sense that anyone would choose a path that comes prepackaged with additional obstacles and potential for harm. Other common retorts to straight people are, "When did you choose to be straight?" and "Can you choose to be attracted to someone of the same sex?" For most human beings, what and who they find sexually attractive is instinctual and automatic. If you find the female form attractive, you know it. And if you find a male form attractive, you know that, too. Maybe you find both attractive. Your body and mind tell you. It's the mind piece that becomes tricky. If your mind also tells you that who and what you find attractive is wrong and will be unacceptable, then you start internalizing shame when your body starts reacting in its normal and healthy way. For some, that internalized shame screams, "You are not gay! You cannot be gay! Do not let anyone know the truth and do everything you can to prove to yourself and everyone else that you are not gay!" And so, for some, pursuing straight relationships and marriages becomes the answer. People who come out later in life are the perfect example of sexuality not being a choice. They tried with all their might to choose to be straight, but nature is not a choice we make.

Sexual Attractions Are Natural, Not a Phase

The second "faulty belief" is that same-sex attraction is just a phase that will go away. I can't count how many times that when a person comes out, people in their lives, especially parents, ask that very question, "Is this just a phase?" Many closeted men stewing in shame want this belief to be real. For many boys, the onset of puberty brings on the dreaded experience of spontaneous erections, which often seem to show up at inconvenient times, like when it's time to line up in class and standing up is the last thing you want to do! The penis seems to truly have a life of its own, detached from anything going on consciously in the mind. At the same time, any sexual thought can cause an immediate reaction, regardless of the exact input, because the thought of anything sexual is new, foreign, and exciting. I offer this data as another point that one can use to hold the belief that one is straight. If when I am first developing, I find the idea of a girl arousing, I must not be gay despite the fact I find the thought of sex with another boy even more appealing. Add to that the reality that sometimes boys do go through "show me yours, and I'll show you mine" experiences with other boys based on curiosity rather than attraction. Curiosity behavior legitimizes the belief that all boys wonder about other boys' bodies and that it has nothing to do with being gay. Finally, young gay men and gay men of any age can find it possible to engage in sex with women that feels good. The fact is that genital stimulation is generally physically pleasurable in any consensual form. If I can perform sexually in opposite-sex situations, then, of course, I am not gay! All of these experiences may validate the idea that one's sexual attraction to other men is indeed just a phase that will pass. With time, the attraction will wane, and by staying committed to a straight relationship, it will go away. Once again, people who go through the very challenging process of coming out later have come to realize that natural sexual attractions will never simply fade away.

Hiding Sexual Identity Only Gets Harder

The next faulty belief we will analyze is that one will be able to manage same-sex attraction while pursuing straight relationships. This belief is one that can initially be weaponized by oneself and by others after a prolonged straight relationship. "You've made it this long; stick it out, buttercup!" Most people find other people who are not their spouse or partner sexually attractive, even when already in a committed and loving relationship. Many people don't like to acknowledge those attractions too openly, but they are real. If a straight man is married, committed, and faithful to a woman despite finding other women attractive and tempting at times, shouldn't a man who feels attracted to other men while married to a woman be able to just control that temptation the same way straight men do with theirs?

Several important factors are missing and ignored in that way of thinking. First, there is a feeling of living authentically and without shame and self-loathing that is impossible when a person is in denial about an aspect of who they truly are. When two people are in a committed relationship, neither would want to know the other struggles with these constant negative feelings about themselves. Likely those feelings come out sideways in anger, sadness, anxiety, or resentments that do not seem to make sense. A person may try to contain, hide, and bury all these feelings, but they come to know that their effort is ultimately futile for all involved.

Another challenge with the "just hang in there" approach is that sex and intimacy will never be complete or fully satisfying when out of alignment with natural sexual identity. If you asked a straight person to never have sex with the opposite sex for their entire life and, instead, only be sexual with the same sex, they would probably not be too on board with that. When a gay person with the best of intentions tries to make a straight scenario work, they will always fall short on the inside no matter how hard they try. A person may see that their partner's feelings are in alignment with self in a beautiful way, and some jealousy can develop about getting to have that experience. Sometimes the sight of that difference leads to horrible self-abuse for not being able to access that experience with someone who loves you so much. Most of my clients report that their sex and intimacy in their marriage felt healthy enough for a while, but as time progressed, sex became more and more of a chore. The "chore" part is less about doing something physically unpleasant but more about the ever-growing anxiety about performance, managing fantasies during sex, and re-experiencing disappointment in their own personal satisfaction and that of their wives. Feeling incomplete in intimacy can inspire shame for falsely letting a loved partner believe that you do reciprocate the same feelings when, in reality, you simply cannot.

Sexual Abuse Has Nothing to Do with Sexual Identity

Some men who come out later in life report a history of sexual abuse in childhood, although they may not use that specific language. They may consider it early sexual activity or play that they feel they consented to, even though they were very young. Others know specifically that they were victimized by predators, and they have the deep emotional scars to prove it. Sometimes people want to explain away same-sex attraction as a consequence of such experiences. Early sexual exposure somehow left an imprint that re-oriented the victim, and if they seek healing for the abuse, they will return to "normal." This misconception is another very difficult and sad faulty belief. Believing abuse is the cause of being gay can prevent someone from stepping out of denial and separating the hurt, shame, and guilt related to sexual abuse from those very similar feelings about being gay. Sexual abuse histories are certainly not overly prevalent in men who come out late; however, it is common enough in the work I have done with clients that it merits some exploration.

Statistics about boys who experience sexual abuse in childhood are hard to measure with an assured accuracy for many reasons. Men and boys tend to report sexual abuse at rates even lower than women and girls. Some men do not apply the definition of sexual abuse to their experiences in childhood and, therefore, would not report them as such. Reports of sexual abuse sometimes are not taken seriously or are ignored out of not wanting a boy to be seen as weak or damaged. General estimates from larger sample analyses assume that a minimum of one in six males experienced sexual abuse in childhood or as an adult. Criminal statistics show that one in fifty-three boys experience physical and violent sexual abuse at the hands of an adult. It is impossible to know the true numbers, but it is inescapable that early sexual experiences or abuse can lead to confusion at the least and significant mental health issues at worst.

The other very dangerous faulty belief is that gay men are perpetrators, out to find boys to sexually abuse. Such an assertion is categorically false, homophobic, and downright hateful. Adults who experience sexual attraction to children are pedophiles, plain and simple. Those who act on those desires are sexual predators deserving of legal consequences. Pedophiles may identify as straight, gay, or anywhere in between. There is simply no credible research or evidence to support the idea that gay men are any more dangerous to children than anyone else. There are some anti-gay groups that try to amplify this myth with invalid or misinterpreted research, but no credible researcher or mental health professional would support such a proposition.

One common denominator in sexual perpetrators is that they look for targets who appear weak and vulnerable, as they may be more likely to never tell. For younger boys who may already be struggling to understand why they behave or feel different from other boys, a predator may see an opening. Most predators are not strangers but usually family or friends of family who have purview into a child's circumstances. That boy who feels like an outsider and different is more likely to appreciate some attention, which can be the grooming of a predator. It is also important to note that a predator has no age requirement. They may be an elderly person or a teenager. Regardless of the age, the impact is often the same: welcomed attention, unwelcomed abuse, and threats to obtain secrecy. For the child, the experience can induce intense confusion, extreme fear, and deep shame and guilt. As that child grows, if they come to realize that their own attraction is for the same sex, those attractions may tap into their confusion, fear, shame, and guilt from those early sexual exposures. At this point, their sexual attraction and abuse history may be knitted together. Such connections support denial and shame about themselves with little insight or even vocabulary to process these complex intersections.

I experienced sexual abuse in separate incidences from family friends when I was between the ages of three and eight. One threatened to kill me if I ever told anyone, and I believed him. Those experiences were violent and brutal, and they left me traumatized in ways that would take decades to unpack. The memories left me terrified of my own natural attraction as I became aware of it as a teenager. The idea of two males sexually connected, much less affectionately attracted, was infused with so much fear and pain. I was already praying regularly to not feel these attractions for all the standard reasons but also because they triggered these memories and feelings. Sexual abuse became one of the buttresses that held up my denial about who I was and who I wanted.

I began experiencing intense flashbacks and panic in my late thirties, and I sought help to understand what was happening to me. Diving into these memories was very hard but ultimately freeing. Without taking time to understand what happened and what it exactly was, I do not think I would have ever found the courage to be honest with myself and others. It was not until I finally separated the abuse and subsequent PTSD that I was able to realize that my natural setting and sexual identity were for other men and that this setting and identity were not bad, scary, or dangerous things. This separation of experiences began my process of accepting myself and pursuing change and authenticity.

I share my personal experience here to illuminate how this particular history interplays with all the other ways men support denial about themselves. Again, not all men who come out late have similar stories, not by far. But for those who do, it is of utmost importance to seek professional help to process and work to heal from a history of sexual abuse. Such work will bear fruit and freedom on the other side.

Coming Out Opens Up Possibilities

Another component I want to examine as part of the why and how of understanding coming out late is what I call the "Armageddon Factor." The perceived cost related to coming out impacts every gay person's decisions about the whens and hows of coming out. Those perceived costs, if not outweighed or at least balanced with perceived benefits, can leave the view of the future with very few possibilities. A young person today may consider the fallout with family (Will I be rejected and maybe kicked out of my house?) and with peers (Will I be bullied and humiliated at school and on social media?). Between family and peers, the cost may be perceived, rightly or wrongly, as an end to their world—Armageddon.

For people who built straight relationships, the perceived losses add up quickly and exponentially, creating a sense of hopelessness and entrapment. Suddenly, the list of potential costs behind this amplified Armageddon Factor grows very long, and the fear of such losses becomes paralyzing:

> Will I hurt my wife deeply and irrevocably to the point that she will never recover or even choose to harm herself or me?
> Will I sentence my children to the horrors of a broken home and the total embarrassment of having a gay parent?
> Will my greater family reject me forever for both being gay and for not seeing the truth for so long?
> Will my friends run screaming from me, never to return?
> Will I lose my job and all I have worked for professionally?
> Will I live in financial ruin and end up homeless and alone?
> Will my church and God cast me out eternally?
> Will I be responsible for not only destroying my world but destroying the worlds of all the people I love?

When gripped with fear and hopelessness, the only answer to all of these questions that a person can see is YES! And so, they stay in place with ever-growing fear and with hopelessness at their core. They also remain ignorant of the incredible evolution that can happen on the other side. One simple example comes from a client who came out later after being divorced from a woman for many years. He fell in unrequited love with his best friend, prompting him to start the journey of coming out. Eventually, he met and married another man and established a new life in Atlanta. At one point in the process, he shared that his mother and his partner's mother met and became fast friends. At the beginning of self-discovery, he could only see possible loss and had no idea that his courage would expand his world and the worlds of those he loved.

It Is Never Too Late

The final faulty belief we will unpack is the idea one is just too old to "start over." Many subscribe to a belief that after forty, fifty, or beyond, it is just too late to be able to rebuild a life and find any kind of peace and happiness after coming out. Perhaps the financial impact of coming out implies a life of poverty and limited means. The greater belief is often that no one will ever want to date an "old man" who carries so much baggage, and the only option is to live and die alone. Once again, fear makes the worst possible result seem likely when, in fact, it is one of the least probable outcomes.

Anyone who experiences life-altering changes later in life (loss of a job, loss of a home, loss of a relationship) knows that the transition is harrowing. Establishing a new normal takes time and effort, but all of the lessons of life learned so far become resources to weather this storm. Let's first consider the fears about the financial future. For one who has been married, going through a divorce and separating finances and assets usually does lead to a change in lifestyle. There is no way around that. Many of the men I have worked with rented apartments during the first phase of this transition as finances and family arrangements got resolved. Such a change may be a significant diminishment of their standard of living. As divorce agreements are reached, a clearer picture of overall financial resources and obligations becomes clearer. At that point, a person can start to adjust financial planning for the future that helps them create what is possible as they move forward. While making adjustments to a standard of living may feel costly at first, new freedoms and possibilities also ensue that can give balance to the financial cost. Perhaps retirement plans are adjusted, or new professional opportunities are pursued to create more stability, but those changes can also bring about new valuable experiences that cannot be seen at first. In the end, it is more likely that the initial financial cost is a detour to a new life that can be even more fulfilling in the long run.

The greater fear usually is that love and relationship will never be found after coming out. Sometimes, that fear is rooted in the faulty belief that gay men simply are not capable or interested in relationship and commitment. More often, that fear is rooted in a belief that an older man is washed up and will be unwanted. Those narratives could not be farther from the truth. First of all, many gay men, like all men, may have been through multiple relationships in adulthood while learning about themselves and what really matters to them. Perhaps it has taken having their heart broken a couple of times for them to really assess what they want and value. Much like a person who comes out later, they have evolved and hopefully done the work to know what they would like in a committed relationship. Are there some gay men who truly do not want to find a partner in life and prefer being single and independent? Of course, there are, and that is true for all people. Are there also many gay men who long for someone who is willing to do the hard work of commitment to get the rewards of a long-term relationship? Yes, there are. In this respect, men who come out later after a marriage often have the asset of knowing about what commitment and sustaining a relationship really involves, and they are more skilled and ready to make that commitment in earnest.

There are many men of all ages who find older men very attractive. Sometimes that attraction is physical, sometimes emotional, and sometimes financial, to be honest. Relationships with an age difference can be healthy or unhealthy, like any relationship. Many newly out men are shocked to find that younger men want to pursue relationships with them. Some men who come out late have a fixated attraction for younger men. They say they only find young, fit men attractive, and they feel no desire for someone more like themselves. Once they are free to explore relationships that are more than sexually based, they come to realize that sustained attraction only happens with multiple levels of compatibility that have little to do with specific age.

One other aspect of attraction is that everyone has certain types that appeal to them. When coming out, a person is simply identifying which gender they prefer at a very high level. Gay men do not find all men attractive; they find some attractive. Sometimes straight friends will suggest that their newly out friend should date another gay person they know simply because they are both gay, with little thought as to whether they have anything else in common. Gay culture, just like straight culture, presents some physical attributes, such as youth and fitness, as the ideal. In reality, again, just like in heteronormative circles, specific tastes and physical attraction run the gamut. My partner sometimes states that there is a lid for every jar, and he is not wrong. People are often surprised to learn that all the things about themselves that they perceive as physical faults may be the very things that someone else finds attractive. In the end, it is just important to know that many unforeseen possibilities exist that eventually teach that this fear of not being attractive enough is simply unfounded.

In work I have done, I have seen many people find love and relationship at any age that is rewarding and long-lasting. I worked with couples who met and married in their sixties and seventies. Two people can meet, fall in love, and grow a relationship regardless of age and circumstances. Sometimes, those relationships that start later in life can be uniquely rich and deep because they are formed by all that came before.

Chapter 5:
INCAPACITATING ANXIETY

This letter was written by a man who started his coming-out process in his early fifties after twenty-one years of marriage and fathering two sons. His fear of hurting others was paralyzing for many years, but with the help and encouragement of friends who loved him, he was able to start to build an authentic and peaceful life.

Dear Me,

I remember where you are. Fear—overwhelming and paralyzing fear consumes you. It is an incapacitating terror. I know in this very anxious place, you see no apparent way forward. While you intellectually understand the beauty of becoming true to yourself by accepting who you are, you simply see no way "out."

You have waited a lifetime to deal with this by always trying to do the "right" thing. It is in the desire to do "right" by others that you have trapped yourself. You worry about the pain you will cause your kids and your wife. You fear the disappointment of your parents. You look at the family pictures on the wall, and you cry. The longer you have waited, the deeper and deeper the hole that traps you has grown. Your feelings are all secondary to the perceived "happiness" of others.

While the fear of hurting others and an unknown future consumes you, there is an equal fear growing ever louder. The fear you will face your death without having had the courage to tackle your own sexuality is becoming even more dreadful. The thought of dying without having faced your sexuality leaves a devastating pit in your stomach at night. All these thoughts run round and round the hamster wheel in your mind, leaving you stuck in a well of incapacitating anxiety. The faster the thoughts spin, the more you feel trapped. An emotional crisis is building within you. Your own mind is your prison, and it is the best jailer ever.

There is a path forward. Of course, telling a story in retrospect is so much easier than facing one in prospect with an uncertain outcome. With an uncertain future, your mind races with so many possibilities, from catastrophe to hope. But there remains a path forward. How do you do it? Honestly, there will be days you will still wonder how you ever did.

The answer for you will lie in the kindness of others, in the friends you will make who will slowly build your courage to change your life. The friends who you met online anonymously, when you were so closeted that it was all you could be, will slowly become real. They will patiently encourage you to take small steps forward. They will listen to you stress and run your anxious thoughts round and round.

Your very first steps will come from the strength found in the love, kindness, and support of these friends. They will encourage you to find a therapist. This help will greatly further your journey. Your therapist will have a support group. As a completely closeted man, you will find the courage to attend. Through that group, your circle of friends will continue to grow further. While the discussions within the support group will have meaning, for you, it is the development of the friendships that will be the most important in the end. Your online and your therapy-led support group friends will become more present for you in real ways.

You will still feel very trapped and will see no progress most days. Feeling so overwhelmed, you will only look for the very smallest of steps forward you can take week by week: little things from going out with new friends for coffee to reading a book to even going to a gay bar. You will focus your thoughts like a laser on the little steps so as not to be consumed by the overwhelming larger task and fear. Without realizing it, as your friendships grow, you will become stronger. You will be inspired by the courage you see in your friends as they travel similar paths.

Then one day, you will name and view your fear as a literal object in your mind—something you have to punch through. Without knowing an outcome, you will tell your parents you want a divorce, and then, with even more effort, you will tell them you are gay. To your relief, you will be greeted with love and support. Your sister will also stand by you. You will cry. Catharsis—you have waited a lifetime to deal with this. You will tell your wife, and there will be pain. There is a cost. You will lastly tell your kids, the one love you cannot lose. To your amazement, your sons will stand up, hug you, and tell you that your revelation "took courage, and they are proud of you." They will tell you that they "love you and want you to be happy." They will also tell their mom they "love her, too, and that she is a strong woman, and she will be okay." You will be in awe of the love and maturity of your teenage boys. It will be one of the proudest, most moving moments of your life.

You will cross to the other side, but there will still be large doubts. You will have arrived at this place with no actual gay sexual experience. You know intuitively who you are, but you will not see any real future. The divorce process will take time and will be emotional. The costs will be real. There will be ups and downs trying to date as an older man. There will even be unexpected setbacks. But the people you meet in your new life will be so interesting and fascinating. You luckily will see humor and joy in your new life. Your friendships will be intense and bound by a depth obtained in your ability to be truly vulnerable and authentic. They will mean the world to you and will have a lifelong quality. And yes, there will even be a boyfriend and love.

Life is short. It is only life, after all. You have to try and live it. You will come to see that doing the "right" thing comes from within the space of being authentic. You will make peace with your shortcomings. Life is messy and full of compromises. While you will regret having missed your sexual youth, you will be comforted by the joy and gift of your children. One of your greatest hopes will be for your children to learn from your mistakes.

In the end, it will take so many to help you. You will need the love of others. This is very difficult stuff, hard stuff, so hard to do alone. You can't begin to get that help until you can take the smallest of steps forward.

While life is not perfect, there is peace with being authentic. It simply does not get any better than that kind of peace.

Chapter 6:
WHAT TRIGGERS CHANGE?

Many forces develop that lead any person to come out, but what happens that drives someone who may be in a straight marriage with children to make the decision to come out and begin a process of change? In my practice, I had clients who felt like they were coming out late in their twenties, and I had clients who came out in their seventies, literally after waiting for their parents to die. That's how terrifying the idea of telling their parents was for them. Some have been in heterosexual marriages, while others never married but also never pursued relationships with other men at all. Some had same-sex encounters along the way, while others never had intimate contact of any kind with another man. The more typical profile of my out-late clients is men between the ages of forty and fifty-five who are or were married, and many of them are fathers. While every story is certainly unique, there are three main identifiable situations that may precipitate making a change, as well as typical and predictable lifespan development influences.

The first situation that can occur is having same-sex drive discovered through basically "getting caught" pursuing same-sex experiences either online or in person. The second is falling in love with another man for the first time and realizing that the love they feel for a spouse or female partner is real but different from what love in alignment with sexuality feels like. The last, which is usually present with the first two, is when the anxiety and depression related to holding this secret reaches a breaking point emotionally and psychologically. Any one of these situations is enough to push someone into action in one way or another, and we will examine them each more closely. The final consideration is related to reaching the time of life when anyone starts looking backward at what has been while considering what they want for the rest of their years, more commonly known as a mid-life crisis.

Getting Caught

Do closeted men have sex with other men outside of their straight relationships with women? For some, it is part of their journey, and for others, it is not. Infidelity from monogamy can and does happen in any type of relationship, gay, straight, or otherwise. I am not trying to minimize the consequences of infidelity but adding context as we explore infidelity by closeted men. Cheating is not unique to any sexual or gender identity. Having added that caveat, let's look more closely at the thoughts and feelings that closeted men often use to rationalize their same-sex behaviors while married or attached to a woman, while at the same time acknowledging that such thinking is rooted in "faulty beliefs" that keep someone in denial and in the closet.

Sexual drive and sexual attraction are natural for most human beings, and denying them totally can lead to all kinds of frustrations and emotional perils. Most people have a private internal call to seek out sexual satisfaction in alignment with their natural sexual attractions, otherwise known as being horny. Couples in a committed, monogamous relationship seek to attend to their needs with each other. Likely they also take time to address their fantasies and desires through masturbation. Most couples, in my experience, choose not to discuss their solo play, and they can even hold their partner in contempt for such behavior. The majority of heterosexual couples who practice monogamy understand the boundaries of their sexual behavior, and stepping outside of those boundaries is understandably a deep break of trust.

A common theme that underpins many closeted men's thinking when it comes to pursuing gay sexual experiences is what I call "apples and oranges." They feel that having sex with a man versus a woman is a very different experience, so they rationalize that acting on their attraction to men is also different. Many never have and never would have sex with another woman outside their primary relationship, but somehow, having sex with another man is perceived as not really cheating. Clearly, this rationalization is false because a commitment to monogamy is a commitment to monogamy. Such a distinction is really built to sustain denial about sexual identity. "I can have sex with another man, but I make love to my wife." Once this distinction leads to sexual encounters with other men, however, the wheels begin their inevitable turning until a person either confesses or gets caught.

Many closeted men do everything in their power to avoid emotionally intimate relationships with other men, even in friendships. By seeking same-sex experiences that are for "sex only," they again rationalize that they are not being emotionally unfaithful, which is somehow better in their estimation. With the advent of the internet, more and more married men started to discover connections with other married men via chatrooms and the like who had the same struggle. Those connections opened the door to possible physical contact with another person in the same boat with just as much to lose. That commonality felt somehow safer, both physically and emotionally, to step into physical encounters. As technology progressed, the birth of hook-up apps such as Grindr and Scruff made finding no-strings-attached sexual encounters extremely easy and, at times, addictive.

A typical scenario is that a man becomes obsessed with fantasies and temptations to the point that he acts out sexually, followed by extreme guilt, shame, and promises to himself to never do it again. The cycle, though, simply starts over on repeat. First, it is a faint call; then, it progresses to a loud drumbeat demanding action. Living with the cycle of that irrepressible call is maddening and fuels the anxiety and depression that amplify over time. Eventually, everyone is discovered at some point if they do not find the courage to come out for themselves. Telling oneself anything else is foolhardy. My clients always believed that they would never be found out. Do some men push the envelope so hard because, deep down, they really want to get caught to just bring it all to an end? Absolutely they do but mostly on a subconscious level.

The reality is that, yes, some closeted men break their vows. Their life-long expertise in maintaining denial, and all the psychological tools that denial employs, creates a cover and explanation for their unfaithful behavior as they try to manage their inner turmoil. Cheating is cheating, however, and in the process of change, they will come to recognize the extent of the ways they hurt their spouse and themselves along the way.

Another common experience of men who step out of their marriage to explore sex with other men is the paranoia related to getting caught and the lengths they go to maintain their secrecy. Suddenly, a person's phone, tablet, laptop, or even family computer becomes the key to exploration and the very thing that can lead to discovery. Changing passwords frequently, having a secret phone, clearing browser histories, multiple secret email accounts, gym memberships and attendance that lead to no change in physical condition, and having ready excuses on hand at any time to cover anything that might slip through—these become anxiety-inducing obsessions that will eventually collapse when unchecked.

Just when I think I've heard every possible way someone's hidden sexual activity may be discovered, I hear yet another new and unexpected scenario. Some of the more common situations are finding gay or bisexual porn on a computer or phone or discovering an unfamiliar email address with graphic emails. In some situations, a secret sexual partner who becomes attached or jealous of a closeted man will out him directly to his wife, family, or even co-workers. And in some cases, a wife walks in unexpectedly to find her husband having sex with another man in their own bed. Needless to say, these types of discoveries are devastating and lead to a bomb going off in life. Sometimes in this situation, a straight spouse can be in such initial shock or denial of their own that they will accept that their husband's same-sex activity was a one-time thing and not emblematic of being gay. For others, it is all the impetus they need for change. In such a state of hurt feelings, sometimes spouses take the step to out their closeted spouse to family and everyone they know. Others feel such shame and embarrassment that they don't want anyone to know. Regardless of the immediate fallout, getting caught always leads to the first steps of making change and coming out.

Falling in Love

Many closeted men have a long history of avoiding emotional connections to other men in general. They don't maintain close friendships with other men, and they sometimes feel more comfortable having female friends. The idea of being emotionally vulnerable and connected to another man seems too risky when trying to tamp down their inner drives. Avoidance of deeper connection does not mean they cannot connect on a fraternal and jovial level with other men, although many closeted men avoid that as well. Most of my clients, but not all, rarely ever had a best male friend to share deeper confidences with since early childhood.

Sometimes a deeper connection can develop, however, and lead someone to discover a nature of love they have never felt. Those feelings may develop for another gay or closeted man, or they may develop with a straight friend. Perhaps a closeted man has engaged in connecting with other gay or closeted men, and one man on one particular day sets off never before felt fireworks. Perhaps a regular friendship, over time, deepens with real emotional intimacy that has never been cracked before. Whatever the precipitating encounter may be, suddenly they feel butterflies in their stomach around this person, think about them all the time, and fantasize about them. They want to spend more and more time with them and make attempts to look as attractive as possible in fitness or presentation. They may not have the ability yet to name this feeling, but they have fallen in love in a way that is in alignment with their true selves for the first time. That feeling, which most men have tried their hardest to avoid all their lives, is as terrifying as it is intoxicating when closeted and married.

One client was divorced for a number of years from his wife, and he developed a very close friendship with a straight couple in his community. He became regularly involved with them and their children, and the kids referred to him as an uncle. He and the male in the couple would stay up some evenings talking deep into the night about any number of things. They were truly best friends. My client, however, became increasingly attracted emotionally and physically to him. The feeling intensified to the point that he had thoughts of ending his life because he could not imagine telling them and possibly losing their relationship. Through work in therapy, he was able to start to know, accept, and love the fact that he was gay. After reaching a place of peace with his sexual identity, he shared his truth with these friends. Acceptance showed up from the beginning, but distance started to grow from both sides as my client began to live openly and pursue relationships. Eventually, he found and married a wonderful man, and his life became full, active, and filled with many new people. He remained friends with the couple that had been centered in his closeted life, but he found the freedom to engage the rest of his life in a way that provided more balance, connection, and personal reward than had ever been in his life before.

Exploring the topic of falling in love opens up the delicate conversation about whether a man ever really loved his spouse or partner. I have yet to work with someone who did not feel deep and abiding love on some level for their straight partner, at least at some point. When someone is in denial about who they are, and they are craving love and a relationship, developing love for someone of the opposite gender is real and the only love they have ever let themselves feel and explore. As that love grows and deepens, it looks like the same kind of love their spouse feels, further confirming that the fear of being gay is unfounded. A gay man can love a straight woman with all that they have available, given the circumstances. If that same man gives himself the opportunity and subconscious permission to fall in love with another man, whoever that man may be, he begins to realize that the love he feels for his wife is something different. It is real and true love but more familial at its core than romantic. He may never have been able to see that without this new experience. If that realization happens, the person can no longer hold up the foundation of his denial. He is forced to see that his sexual attractions are true, fixed, and unchangeable. He then has the choice to come out more consciously or continue to hide his true self. The "Armageddon Factor" can kick in here, leading him to choose to stay hidden for fear of the consequences. In any event, his new understanding of love and himself also may begin the process of change and self-acceptance.

Emotional Overwhelm

The last situation that leads someone to come out later in life is usually embedded under all of the other forces. The feelings of anxiety and depression related to keeping this secret generally grow and grow over time. A person sees themselves as terrible not only for being gay but for the choices they have made along the way to hide and run from that reality. Most Out-Laters feel much more guilt and shame about having lied to people than they do about their sexuality. These feelings can become overwhelming and spill out in ways that seem inexplicable. Spouses and families can be puzzled about what's causing such unhappiness. Family members may start to question themselves and think that if they were better in some way, the person they love would be happier.

Anger, panic attacks, job struggles, and isolation set in for some in profound ways. Anxiety often shows up with physical symptoms like panic that feel like a heart attack, general physical pain, uncontrolled racing thoughts, memory struggles, and/or upset stomach that medicine won't help. Some may seek medical attention for these symptoms and come up empty-handed as to a cause. Good doctors will ask about anxiety and stress, but if a person is in such fear and denial that they can't give voice to their sexual struggles, they will often attribute it all to more acceptable stressors such as work. And so, the wheel of anxiety spins even faster as a person will beat themselves up more for not having the courage to speak or see the truth.

Depression, like anxiety, is a horrible disease that lies to people. In an out-late situation, depression often tells a person that they have made so many mistakes and are so damaged that there is no way out. I have had clients who reached out to me for the first time after spending some very scary times holding a gun in their hand or making a noose out of a belt or sheet—desperate to end their own pain and wanting to spare their loved ones from knowing the truth. I experienced similar feelings in my own journey. Not long after coming out and divorcing, I sank into a prolonged and profound depression. I believed that I had done nothing but cause irreparable harm to those I loved most and that any further exposure to me would only cause more harm. Although I was certain losing me would be difficult, in the depths of my depression, I believed they would be better off in the long run. I was so very wrong about that, and I luckily had the help and support of professionals and family to get me through that very troubling time.

We have no way of knowing how many people never reached out for help and took the step of ending their lives instead of speaking the truth, but there are many. Studies from the American Journal of Preventative Medicine indicate that gay men are four to five times more likely to attempt suicide than straight men. I know one woman whose husband died by suicide, and she later found out that one of his struggles was being gay and hiding it. He never told her anything about it, and she learned about his sexual struggle through a friend. Although this new piece of information did not resolve her immense pain and loss, nor did it fully account for the entire depression her husband felt, knowing this new information made what seemed so puzzling make a little more sense. She told me that she would give anything to have a gay ex-husband, for his children to have a gay dad, rather than to have them all live the rest of their lives without him.

Clearly, coming out while in a straight marriage results in pain, anxiety, and depression for all involved. An easy and painless option does not exist. In the end, however, the old adage "the truth will set you free" is real and the most loving and selfless path a person can choose. If, in reading this book, you find yourself in a place of emotional overwhelm at the prospect of coming out, if the option of dying seems more palatable than the option of honesty, please reach out for help as soon as possible:

> ➤ The Trevor Project is a non-profit that works to support LGBTQ+ youth and prevent suicide, and their hotline number is 866-488-7386.
> ➤ The National Suicide Prevention Lifeline is 800-273-8255.
> ➤ You can call 988, a new emergency mental health number that includes options for LGBTQ+ support.

➤ You can call 911 or go to an emergency room for help.

➤ Reach out to a trusted friend.

➤ Start researching a counselor to call who can help.

Relief and possibilities are available and around the corner, so hold on and seek assistance as soon as you can. It is not an exaggeration that the emotional toll of staying in the closet can become a life-and-death situation for anyone. For those who come out later, it is often these very real and present thoughts of finding some alternative escape from inner torture that begin the process of change.

Lifespan Development

As I noted earlier, the typical age range of clients I see is between forty and fifty-five. We are all familiar with the idea of the "mid-life crisis." A rudimentary example often portrayed in popular media would be a middle-aged dad who buys a sportscar or motorcycle to try to recapture youth or excitement. In reality, this cliché is actually addressing a typical and normal stage of life that many go through when they start to understand that their life is not going to last forever; in fact, it is likely around the halfway point. During middle age, many people spend some time examining how they got to where they are in terms of relationships, family, community, and work. They also start planning for the future to determine what they still want to accomplish and what has the most meaning and value to them as they move into the second act of life. Most importantly, they examine what changes, if any, they want to make to enjoy the most of their time and gifts.

For some, this examination may lead to a career change. For others, it may mean a change in geographic location. And for others, it may mean a change in primary relationship if what they have is not what they'd hoped for or what they want for their future. Many straight couples divorce during this season of life with the belief that they at least have time to start over relationally. When a person is deeply closeted and tormented by hiding themselves, they also start to entertain the idea of coming out and living a life where they can finally show up consistently across all spectrums of life as their whole self. They, too, feel the pull of needing to make a change while they still can create a future that is in alignment with who they are. This aspect of lifespan development also precipitates change, and the other situational events we've looked at often occur due to this natural evolution in how all people examine their past and future.

Section Two:
GETTING OUT

Chapter 7:
ACCEPTANCE OF SELF AND THE JOURNEY

I am gay. In my work, I have been honored and humbled to be the first person to whom someone has ever said those words out loud. That moment is usually infused with a wash of relief and a wash of panic at the same time. With those words, a person takes his first baby steps in the coming-out process. Sharing it with a counselor in a private session is at once monumental and also just a test run. Contemplating the day when it is shared with others in real life can be terrifying, as that becomes the step from which there is no turning back. We will next explore some overall expectations and themes that unfurl in the coming-out process. I divide this experience into three phases. The first is the actual process of coming out later to self and others and the resulting consequences for identity, as well as for family and community systems. The second is adapting to being out and perhaps single again in a community that can be pretty intimidating and unfamiliar at first. The final step is what I term "Coming True." This final stage is when sexual identity and the role it plays are fully integrated and even celebrated across all spectrums of life.

I once again want to step on a soap box of sorts for a moment and lament the idea that coming out is necessary at all. We are raised and live in a society with a presumption of straightness. Being straight is the expected default setting. Straight people never have to fret about when and how to tell others about their sexual identity. They actually never have to tell anyone. Instead, they just pursue their lives and relationships without fear of family or societal rejection. Imagine, if you will, a world where parents hold onto hopes for their kids that someday they will enjoy love, relationship, family, and purpose, but they never once presume who their child will or should love. Instead of anyone ever "coming out," they simply start dating and relating in the way they are made without fear of consequence or judgment. I like to imagine such a world, but that is not the world we live in today, not yet anyway. So, we who identify with any sexual or gender minority participate in this ritual and shared experience of coming out.

Process of Coming Out

You probably know from reading so far that I love some definitions! Words matter, and having a common understanding is pretty essential to be able to connect to concepts. Coming out is a process, not an event. There is not one day when a person makes a declaration, and then they are "out." It evolves over time and, in some ways, never stops. In writing this book, I am still coming out to new people who have never heard of me. Whenever gay, bi, or anything in between folks, meet new people in life, at some point, their history and identity become revealed—either directly in conversation or through observation of whom they love and how they live. In that sense, the "coming out" never really ends. It just becomes more self-evident rather than an action one takes.

When a person has identified as straight through word and deed for a long time in adulthood, the coming-out process, already hard, becomes even more complicated as it challenges the conceptions that family and friends hold about a person based on their adult choices. One of the comforts on the other side of the coming-out process is the addition of new people in a person's life that will only know them as gay—no disclosures or shifting identity to explain. Another comfort that can serve as a bonding mechanism in their new community is the sharing of coming-out stories. The stories are as varied and unique as each person, but what unifies us is that we all have one.

The coming-out process begins when one chooses or is forced to step out of denial and deception and into acceptance. For those coming out later, that acceptance is of self and the journey it took to reach such a point. The latter is usually a much tougher row to hoe, but we will begin by looking at what it means to be accepting of self. Recall the definition of gay as an internal setting that says one is primarily sexually and affectionately attracted to the same gender. For many men, sexual attraction is self-evident and somewhat easier to name and accept as true. It is the affectional attraction that may seem foreign and new and therefore harder to see as fact.

Affectional attraction means feeling love, intimacy, desire, and romance for someone else. Think of it as holding hands, cuddling, kissing, or sharing pillow talk. When deeply in the closet, those actions may feel like a step too far—or actually a step too dangerous. Many closeted men actively avoid expressing affection with another man, even if they are sexually intimate. They may feel and behave in sexually uninhibited ways with other men but refuse to kiss. These seemingly odd boundaries in behavior are rooted in feelings of shame and self-loathing about their true self. Their negative narrative kicks in loud and clear and drowns out what is usually a true desire for the whole package. Given a history of avoiding such affection, it is understandable that admitting a need for such a connection is scary for some. Seeing two men walk down a street holding hands may more closely align with what their heart really wants, as it represents freedom from hiding, but it may also trigger worrying about what others think, which is the foundation of the shame that has been like a two-ton boulder they've been carrying for a long time.

The first step of self-acceptance is only that. It does not mean anyone has to jump on what feels like a fast-moving runaway train. It simply means accepting one's sexual identity as true and unchangeable. Often in life, one of the hardest things to do is accept something we don't like. Just because a person is ready to accept that they are gay does not mean they have to immediately like that fact about themselves. But it is vital to understand that it is only one fact about who they are. It does not change all the other aspects of self and one's character. When a person finally states, "I am gay," it can feel like a big neon sign lights up on their forehead saying "GAY!" It does step to the forefront of thought and self-examination for a while, and it often leads to changes in the structure of one's life. In that sense, it can feel like it defines everything about self at first. It does not define everything, however, and the subsequent journey brings back an equilibrium where one can say, "I am right-handed, I enjoy playing golf, my favorite color is blue, I am gay, I am fascinated with history, my family means the world to me, and I am really good at my job."

The Power of Self-Forgiveness

The greater and usually harder work comes in accepting all that it took to reach this place and time in life. Nearly all my clients had a much harder time accepting the choices they made along the way that hurt people in their lives than they do accepting that they are gay. They feel overwhelming guilt and believe that they are unforgivable to others, much less to themselves. Usually, at some point before they reach a therapist's couch, they are further along in knowing the truth about their sexuality but have continued the charade out of fear, shame, and guilt. Resolving those feelings, or at the very least, learning to hold them in perspective, is essential to healing. When a man feels like all he has done is unforgivable, asking him to start by forgiving himself may seem like a stretch. In reality, some never free themselves from the guilt 100 percent, but they can move forward knowing that they no longer will engage in the behaviors that caused the guilt in the first place. If we start with the idea that forgiving oneself does not have to be an all-or-nothing proposition, then moving toward healing and acceptance of the journey can begin.

Many people use the word "forgiveness" without ever really taking time to understand what it means on a personal level, both operationally and emotionally. Forgiveness is often spoken of as a transaction. "I've done something hurtful, and I am asking for your forgiveness." The person on the receiving end then says, "Yes, I forgive you." In this scenario, forgiveness is something one person gives to another person. How many times, though, does the person who forgives bring that action back up in a moment of anger or dispute? We have all done exactly that, and it would indicate that forgiveness never really happened. We are holding onto the anger or hurt despite our words. What if forgiveness is not given to someone else but something we do for ourselves instead? I describe forgiveness as a path to freedom from the hurt and anger that results from being harmed. It is something we do for ourselves, not for another person.

Forgiveness does not mean acting like nothing ever happened. "Forgive and forget" is as silly as it is impossible. "Forgive and remember, learn, and change" is probably a better adage to adopt. When a person is consumed with guilt and shame for their behavior, moving toward forgiving themselves can be viewed as selfish. After all, guilt and shame are the ways we punish ourselves, and if we hold onto the belief that we deserve punishment more than forgiveness, we cling to them as a sentence that must be served. Healing is actually the path that leads to a place where we can show up and take responsibility for our actions. Healing ourselves is an act of selflessness that allows us to start to show up in the ways those we aggrieved need in order for them to heal. On the path to self-forgiveness, it is vital to remember, learn, and change in ways that will stop the destructive, hurtful things we do to others and ourselves.

That may all sound good enough, but how does a person who is coming out later in life engage in self-forgiveness? First, they take time to analyze the way that family, culture, and perhaps faith influenced the decisions they made along the way. They work to understand their own story that was probably never driven by wanting to hurt anyone but driven instead by trying to do what they thought was right. It also comes from understanding that some of those forces of judgment and discrimination related to being gay played their unjustified role. Lastly, it comes from accepting that it took what it took to break down the denial and fear. It does not matter that some came to a place of self-acceptance earlier or in less consequential ways. It took what it took, and it cannot be rewound or replayed. All that can be done is to move forward. Self-forgiveness then also includes choosing to move forward from this point on in honesty, dignity, and respect for self and others in ways that may have been missing until now. The path to acceptance of self and the journey is neither short nor easy. Self-reflection will deepen and become fruitful with time and nurturance, and it develops alongside the rest of the coming-out process that involves telling the truth and adapting to this new reality. Working on self-forgiveness can be enhanced greatly with individual counseling or therapy.

Chapter 8:
THE RINGS OF DISCLOSURE

The next step in the coming-out process is disclosure. If someone is contemplating self-disclosure, they may freeze at the very idea. The fear of taking an irreversible step can be overwhelming, and that same fear leaves them unable to see the reality that disclosure is just one moment in time followed by life just continuing. For some, disclosure is thrust upon them after being discovered, and it may feel like a nuclear bomb has upended everything they knew. We will take a look at how to manage through either scenario, but we will start with the situation where a person is planning to self-disclose. Not disclosing complicates the opportunity to receive the much more probable love and acceptance that likely may result from family and friends, or at the very least from a new set of people who will become part of a support network.

This process begins with what I call "rings of disclosure." At the very center is the person who shares the center of the family—a spouse

or significant other. Next are the people who have the closest connections and to whom coming out will have the biggest impact. If
children are involved, they are often on the next ring beyond the
spouse, depending on their age and what may be agreed to between
spouses. The next ring usually involves parents and family members,
but it may also include close friends. Think of these inner rings as
the people who most need to hear about coming out directly from
their loved one. The next level may include more friends and possibly
coworkers. It may extend to aunts and uncles, cousins, etc. At some
point, however, this information starts to spread on its own, and the
responsibility for directly coming out to people is no longer necessary.
It's good to think of it as a ripple effect that starts to move out with
a life of its own. Once again, the help of trusted mental health professionals can be valuable in preparing for disclosure conversations.

Before we examine disclosing to the rings of family and close
friends, it is also important to realize that once this information is
shared, the person receiving it has a right to talk about it with others as
well. There may be time-limited requests to hold onto such knowledge
to give the person coming out time to talk to the most important
people in their lives. That request, however, must have an end time.
For the people receiving this news, it becomes part of their own stories
for which they need support. I have a gay spouse. I have a gay son.
I have a gay dad. My brother is gay. Adjusting their understanding
of someone they love is now part of their reality, and they are free to
share this shift with those who will support them. Asking anyone to
keep it a secret only perpetuates the belief that coming out is terrible
news that should be attached to shame. Ultimately the spread of
this knowledge is an essential part of coming out and the renewal of
self-esteem and self-respect.

Telling a Spouse

At its very core, disclosing sexual identity will have the biggest impact on a spouse or partner on all levels, including sex. Clearly, disclosure is ultimately about more than "sexual issues," as one is working to be able to show up authentically in all aspects of life. Let's begin with a man who is married to a woman and is planning to start coming out. How and where to begin? The most important person who needs to be told is one's spouse or partner. They share the center of the family unit, and this disclosure will have the biggest impact on them. Sometimes a person may feel like they need some outside support from a counselor, friend, or family member before they take this step, and that can be helpful. If choosing to share with someone other than a spouse first, it is very important to have trust that such a disclosure will be met with understanding and love. Otherwise, a difficult experience will only increase the fear and avoidance of having what are the most important conversations.

It is not unusual for a person to want to wait for the perfect disclosure moment in order to minimize the immediate fallout. For instance, some say, "Well, I will wait until after the holidays, or after their birthday, or after our kids' birthdays, or after winter is over, or after Flag Day," and on and on. This search for the perfect moment becomes another avoidance mechanism because there is no such thing as a perfect moment. I generally tell people there is no better day than today. I do not mean that they should go home immediately and tell all, just that in the end, the exact day and time will not matter that much. Is telling your wife on Mother's Day or Christmas Day or the like the best idea—of course not. But outside of those occasions, any old day will do.

Some things to consider are based on common sense. Make sure there is time and privacy available. Having this conversation in a public place like a restaurant may seem like it would limit the possibility of a big scene, but the opposite is more likely. The best place is at home or in a private setting where no one will disturb or interrupt. Late at night after kids are asleep is an option, understanding that people tend to become more emotional and irrational when they are already tired. Another consideration is choosing to have this conversation when everyone is sober. Some think a little liquid courage will help get the words moving. People's emotions also tend to amplify after a few drinks, so choosing a time when both are clear-eyed and clear-headed is more ideal. These factors about the setting can be controlled and helpful, but again, understand that the fallout from such a conversation is going to happen no matter where or how it takes place. This initial disclosure will be just the beginning of many conversations that will happen in the coming days and weeks.

As for the conversation itself, finding the right words can also seem challenging and another reason to avoid it. Some find it helpful to write out their thoughts in advance to help guide them through what they want to say. Some literally read what they have written to their spouse to be able to get out all of their thoughts. My recommendation is to stick with mostly "I" statements:

- ➤ I have something very hard to talk about.
- ➤ I have been struggling with this for a very long time, and I am so scared to talk about it.
- ➤ I have to be honest about something that has been very painful.

At least at the beginning, it is important not to telegraph to the spouse what they should be feeling or what they should think. They get to have that all on their own.

Another aspect that is very important is to be very open with emotions. If scared, show it. If hurting, show it. Sometimes a person thinks, "I need to be strong and keep myself together because my spouse is going to fall apart." Disclosure is not a time to hold back tears or sadness. It is of the utmost importance that the person receiving this news can see that it is hard and painful. If this revelation is presented with a calm, cool demeanor, it will come across as something that doesn't matter as much to you as it does to them. It will reinforce any response they may have about you never loving them, etc. Showing your pain and struggle lets them know that opening up about this is important and very difficult. Finally, it is most important that at some point, the essential truth is clearly and unequivocally spoken: I am gay.

Up to this moment, you have some control over what is said and how it is said. After this moment, it becomes a mutual conversation and experience that cannot be predicted with any certainty. It usually begins a roller coaster that you will both ride for quite a while. I will share some more common reactions and experiences I have seen in my work, but know that every situation is unique. Sometimes the initial reaction is way more loving and supportive than one expects. A spouse may state that they love you no matter what and you will get through this pain together. They may be in a state of shock and trying to make sense of what this revelation will ultimately mean. Some spouses have a reaction understandably filled with rage and pain and many, many questions. One may feel a pull to try to sort out an answer completely and quickly when it really needs much time to unfold.

There are some pitfalls in these initial conversations to try to avoid if possible, which we explore next, but there is a very important concept to remember in this moment, as well as in all disclosure moments with family and friends yet to come. This journey likely has taken you decades to work through. You have been working up to knowing and understanding your sexual identity for many years. When you disclose to your spouse or those beyond, it is often their day one. They need and deserve time to work through understanding what this may mean. A person's reaction on day one will be different from day thirty, or in six months, and very different from what it will be in one, five, or ten years. Do not read into or invest truth into initial responses, positive or negative—they will evolve.

As for the potential pitfalls I mentioned a moment ago, the most important thing to be shared is the essential truth about sexual identity. Sharing this important fact does not mean that a person has to disclose every thought, feeling, or deed they have ever experienced related to their journey. If pushed to reveal anything and everything, it is not harmful to be judicious or sparing in this initial revelation. Spouses may immediately want to know every detail about everything that may have ever happened, but they often later regret knowing too much. It is okay to explain that you want to be as honest as you can be and will do so as you both work through this disclosure over time. Some do feel relief in letting out everything, especially if there are things that are going to become known eventually. Hiding them further at this point can be more harmful, but over-disclosing details of names and places can have harmful outcomes for innocent bystanders that can't be seen in the heat of a moment. I understand that this approach is delicate, and there is no one answer that is right for everybody. Just know that efforts to protect someone from hurting more than is necessary are not always bad.

Another pitfall is feeling the need to provide answers about what is going to happen next. Some spouses do immediately take the position that they understand how hard sharing this truth is, but they want to commit to staying together and making it work. When presented with an offer like that in such a terrifying moment, one can feel like they must accept such graciousness. I've told them this monumental thing, and they are being so amazing, so how can I possibly say that I don't think staying together is something that can work? Unless one is certain about what path they want, it is best to remain noncommittal to the outcome but very committed to the process of figuring out together how best to proceed.

A final pitfall is diverting from this disclosure to problems in a marriage that are unrelated to sexual identity. It is not uncommon that people in this situation have multiple problems within their marriage that are part of any marriage that is in trouble. It can be very tempting to bring all of them up and say that sexual identity is only one of many problems, and some of those problems are your fault! That may very well be the reality of the situation, and it may very well become the reality that a spouse will blame all of the marital problems on this one issue and make all of it your fault in their eyes. The narrative that each person walks away with may be different and will take time to develop, but in this moment, it is best to keep the conversation focused on the sexual identity issue. The rest will work itself out in due time.

Once this conversation has unfolded, the sun will rise, and another day of work and family will get underway. More conversations and decisions will happen over the days and weeks ahead. Life will go on, and every hiccup will be handled as they happen. The shared reality within the marriage will be forever changed, but where things end up will be worked out along the way.

It is possible that the initial response will be more fueled by anger and outright hostility. A spouse may ask you to leave and hurl promises that they will destroy you and never let you see your kids again. This response is actually very rare in the work I have done with clients, but it is important to know that giving the space they need to process and calm down to an extent is usually the best choice. The reality is that if a divorce and subsequent custody arrangement are reached, one spouse cannot legally dictate those terms or prevent one parent from seeing their children. Those words usually come from the shock and anger from this revelation and subside in the coming hours and days.

The last scenario that needs to be addressed is the situation where a spouse discovers this truth before it has been disclosed. Unexpected discovery is much more painful for all involved, and the sense and reality of betrayal play a much bigger role. If you are in a situation where you have not disclosed but have the potential for discovery, hearing about the reality of the latter can hopefully be motivation to choose disclosure first. Waiting to be caught only limits the control a person has over how the rest of the story unfolds and makes a civil and respectful outcome harder, though not impossible, to reach.

Those who have been discovered unwillingly have all experienced a truly traumatic experience, albeit of their own making. An over wash of panic and extreme fear, a desire to run away or deny what is true, and even a defensiveness about their behaviors are common responses. That initial unexpected encounter with their spouse and the truth is terrifying but survivable. My best encouragement in that situation is to acknowledge what is known and not to whitewash or diminish what has happened. The defensiveness instinct, as well as an instinct to say whatever it takes in the moment to comfort a spouse, should be challenged internally. Just like self-disclosure, do not be afraid to show emotion and confirm the questions about sexuality. Also, be cognizant that saying much beyond the truth and an apology for the very real pain unfolding will do little to lower the tension in the moment. A time for reflection, understanding, and explanation will come more naturally with taking a little time for calming. Assure a partner that the door is open to talk and work on the consequences of what was discovered, but also know that asking for some time to regroup is not a bad thing for either party. Be prepared to have a place to go for a night, whether in a hotel room or staying with a friend or family member. Also, be prepared to stay and absorb the appropriate angry response if it feels right and safe to do so. In the face of everything, many do feel some small sense of relief that the day they avoided so desperately but somehow knew would come has finally arrived.

Whether disclosure to a spouse is voluntary or involuntary, it is just the beginning of a dialogue to determine what comes next. There is not a one-size-fits-all prescription for a correct outcome. Most marriages, when faced with this issue, do end in separation and divorce. Some couples work to preserve their relationship with the full knowledge that they are in a mixed-orientation marriage, and that presents its own challenges. I wish I could say that I have seen couples flourish under that umbrella, but that is not the case. They find ways to remain married for a variety of reasons, but it often involves living with a given amount of distrust and insecurity related to sexual behavior in and out of the marriage. Some choose to open up the sexual boundaries, but often the straight spouse then has to manage the possibility that by doing so, their loved one could poten-tially fall in love elsewhere. Others commit to renewed monogamy with the best of intentions and numerous new safeguards (no private online access, no spending money separately, etc.), but even then, a certain level of comfort with the real possibility of betrayal must be managed. When considering staying together, it is important that both parties honestly desire it and desire it for the same clear reasons.

Sharing with Parents

I want to repeat something I mentioned in the last section because it is very important to remember as telling people unfolds. This journey likely has taken you decades to work through. You have been working up to knowing and understanding your sexual identity for many years. When you disclose to your spouse or those beyond, it is often their day one. They need and deserve time to work through what this may mean. A person's reaction on day one will be different from day thirty, or in six months, and very different from what it will be in one, five, or ten years. Do not read into or invest truth into initial responses, positive or negative—they will evolve.

What happened when I came out to my parents is a perfect example of the evolution in the reaction that may occur. My former wife and I held this information between us for a couple of months in order to give us time to make some thoughtful decisions about how to move forward. Once we both agreed that staying together was not something either of us wanted (a very painful process, to be sure), it was time to start to share what was happening. We chose to tell our children first (they were fifteen and twelve at the time), and then we wanted to tell immediate family right away so that the kids would not have to keep this information a secret and be able to talk to their grandparents, etc. if they needed to. We were living in Atlanta, and both of our sets of parents were out of state. We called them each separately after talking to the kids. My parents were both on the line together, and the immediate reaction was silence. My mother started by saying she loved me no matter what, that she was shocked, and that she was very sad that this was happening to our family and me. My father remained silent for a long time, and then he said, "William, I don't want to say anything stupid, so I'm not going to say anything at all." I was so scared in this conversation, and that response seemed pretty good under the circumstances.

Several weeks passed until the day he called me back. He said, "Son, I think gay people are the lowest form of life on the planet, and I just can't love you anymore." Wow. Deep breaths and tears welling up. My first thought was, "What was the stupid thing you were going to say because what you are saying now is pretty awful." I stammered through, saying I understood and was sorry he felt that way. We hung up, and I fell apart. The rest of the family had been very supportive and understanding, but that little boy in me who always thought he needed to do whatever would make his dad proud was crushed.

My father felt the wrath of my mother and sisters for what he said. They were ready to banish him from their lives for being so cruel. My father's youngest brother is gay, a secret that was never said out loud but was well known. This brother, my uncle, was beloved by my dad and all of the family. My dad had found a way to love and be close to his brother, but when it came to his own son, it was too much at first. I do not believe he was trying to be cruel to me. I think he was trying to make sense of something that he wished was not true for whatever reasons.

Another thing to know about my father is that he could be a stubborn old mule, and other people could never change his thinking. That always had to happen within himself. After several more weeks and taking time to reflect on all he had learned, he called me once again. This time he said, "Son, you have done nothing in my life but make me proud, and I can't imagine that will ever stop. I am sorry, and I love you." His day one reaction was shock. His day thirty reaction was defiance and judgment. His three-month reaction was acceptance and love. Up until the day he died, he remained loving, kind, and supportive to my family and me.

My story is not to say that negative reactions will always evolve into love and acceptance over time. Sometimes they reach tolerance at best. Telling parents is very tricky and dicey for many. It is not uncommon that a mother is told first, and then she may share the news with the father. Parents hold wishes for happiness and safety for their children, even when they are adults. News like a child coming out can trigger deep fears for parents about what will happen to their son. It may run up against deeply held religious beliefs of their own, leading to intense self-reflection. Until the day comes when a parent can see their gay son in a relationship with another actual male human being, they may have a very hard time truly being able to absorb this new truth, at least in a way that does not seem unsettling. It is also not at all uncommon to hear from parents that they always knew on some level, and seeing their son be able to be honest with himself, them, and the world may be a welcomed relief.

This revelation with parents has unique forces at play, as the fear of telling them has been around much longer than the fear of telling a spouse. Telling a spouse may end in divorce, but telling parents has no formal mechanism in reaction. Stories heard over time of parents rejecting their children forever ring loud in a closeted person's mind. The felt loss of a parent's pride and love can never be replaced or recreated in a new relationship, so the stakes feel extraordinarily high.

Much like disclosure to a spouse, thought and planning can relieve some of the anticipatory fear. As far as the setting goes, if possible, having this conversation with them in their home is preferred, which places them in a surrounding that is safe for them. Such a choice also retains the ability to leave or end the conversation whenever necessary. Once again, keeping language based in "I" statements is best, as well as keeping the sharing simple and direct. They will need time and space to let this information settle. They may or may not have any questions, and they may or may not be very surprised by the news. Assuring them that they can ask questions is helpful, but realize that as time progresses, they may not know how to ask out of fear of saying the wrong thing. I've had several clients who have this monumental conversation with their parents, and then their parents never bring it up again. Clients are often somewhat hurt by this apparent indifference, and they interpret that indifference as judgment. This phenomenon is sometimes referred to as "rebuilding the closet." More often than not, it is simply a hesitance and ignorance about what words to say and what may or may not be a privacy violation. We then begin the role of having to teach the people in our lives that it is okay to talk about it, and we model for them how to talk about it.

Talking to Children

If children are involved, telling them and what to tell them can be one of the hardest nuts to crack. While research about the effect a parent's coming out as gay has on a child is minimal, some studies have looked at the impacts of disclosure at different ages. The results of any study cannot always be applied to broad populations, but the information can still be useful. Research says that younger children tend to incorporate this change more easily than teenagers and much more easily than adult children. Younger children are still learning about people, the world, and themselves, and parents can have a lot of influence on how they interpret this information. Teenagers are in the middle of discovering their own sexual identity and also working to individuate from their parents. They may have very conflicted responses rooted in learning this truth, all the while trying to learn about their own truth. Adult children sometimes have similar questions and reactions to what their straight parent may have: What else have you lied to me about? Was anything ever true? Why are you telling us now? I encourage parents to consult with a professional who works with children or adolescents to gain support on how best to approach their own children, as well as to have a resource for the children to work with if they have difficulty with this change.

If there is conflict between parents about what or when to talk to kids, it is best to take time to see if a place of compromise can be reached. Depending on the straight parent's beliefs, they may want to insist that the information be hidden from the children to protect them from exposure to "the gay lifestyle." Taking time to explore those fears with professional guidance is essential, and agreeing to some timed boundaries may be helpful. In some cases, however, a straight spouse may never agree that sharing a parent's non-straight identity with the children is ever a good idea. The reality is that children are going to discover this truth one way or another and far earlier than expected when it is being kept secret. Children listen, overhear and observe, and if they learn about a parent being gay without permission to talk about it, they are left to struggle with secret keeping. They are also left with messages that being gay is shameful and wrong enough that it must not be addressed. All these messages are ultimately detrimental to the family system and the children themselves. At some point, the parent who has come out may need to take a unilateral step to lovingly and kindly share this information with their children. In such circumstances, the other parent must be told, and resources for support through counseling or the like must be at the ready.

Many are struck deeply with guilt that they will ruin their children's lives forever. Any children in a home that experiences divorce will have some difficulties in the aftermath. Those difficulties are to be expected, and finding them help and support through professionals, teachers, family, and friends is very important. It is also important to know that, on average, children who experience divorce tend to return to similar outcomes as their peers after about two years, according to the book *Parenting Plan Evaluations: Applied Research for the Family Court*. Using this experience to model for children how to face adversity, how to choose truth, and how to be vulnerable can actually be very valuable to them in the long run.

One aspect to be aware of in all disclosure conversations beyond a spouse is that these conversations are often much shorter and less intense than one fears. For instance, when my former wife and I were preparing to share this truth with our children, I had a scenario in my head that this would be a very long and fraught revelation with a seemingly endless outpouring of emotion. In reality, the first conversation itself lasted less than ten minutes. The kids were emotional and had a few questions, but they did not need a great deal of explanation or resolution initially. Those developed over time in many conversations and long hugs that happened in the days, weeks, and even years that followed.

What children need most of all is to know that they are loved and cared for and that it is not their fault. They also need to not only be reassured but also witness that their mom and dad will be able to take care of themselves in all this change. They may feel the pull to try and take care of their parents, who are obviously hurting as well, and it is incumbent that they know that everyone will be okay and that Mom and Dad are getting good help to make sure of it. It is also helpful to make sure they know that the decisions Mom and Dad make around the future will always put their well-being and care above all else. Even if these things seem far from true in the moment when Mom and Dad are actually pretty terrified and unsure what is going to happen, creating a space of safety to talk and feel is paramount for them. Just like with other disclosure conversations, it is okay not to have all the answers to their questions, but it is a must that they know that they are loved and will be cared for by their mom and their dad.

Approaching Family and Friends

The next round of conversations we will consider is with extended family and friends. A person may choose to go in any order that seems right for their situation, but it is usually the closest family connections that may seem the most daunting. Once these initial conversations take place, time needs to pass for all to adjust, and more in-depth talk can happen over time. The first element to consider is that in sharing this news, we are starting to teach those we love how to talk about having a gay person in their lives. If the disclosure is steeped in shame, we are teaching them that this topic is shameful and should be treated that way. Some feel an impulse to preface the news with statements like, "I know you are going to be hurt and disappointed" or "I know you are going to be angry." These messages telegraph what they should feel, even if they don't. It is perfectly alright to share that you are scared or nervous, but that is just sharing your own feelings and not dictating what their response will be. As strange as it may sound, coming out is ultimately good news that you have moved into being fully honest and open with yourself and with them. The road ahead may be rocky for a while, but it hopefully ends in a better place for all. I encourage holding at least an internal posture that coming out is a good and positive step no matter how difficult it may be.

Additional steps can be taken to try to manage getting through these conversations as smoothly as possible. First, it is again best to have these talks in a place of privacy and a place that is comfortable for them. The other aspect to consider is having this conversation when there is either a natural endpoint or at least a natural change of topic. If you are going to have a meal together, for instance, have the conversation before starting, so the meal becomes a natural action that changes the topic and experience. For some friends and maybe family where the fear of negative reaction is lower, maybe meet at a restaurant where a check will come, and natural goodbye will take place. Certainly, be prepared for some questions, but also know that "I don't know" is a perfectly reasonable response. Try to be as honest as possible, but it is not required that you have concrete answers to every inquiry. Saying that you are in the process of understanding what all coming out will mean and don't have all the answers is the truth. Remember also that you still have a right to privacy. No one is entitled to know every detail about your journey, and keeping some aspects appropriately private is very different from keeping secrets.

As the rings may expand to neighbors and more casual friends, most people actually do not want to know too much. Just mentioning that a separation or divorce is coming is enough for some. Many people hold some fear inside about their own marriages and relation-ships, and when confronted with someone else's issues, they will offer sympathy but feel reluctant to dive too far into the details. As more conversations take place over time, it becomes easier and easier, and it is natural to develop an elevator speech version of the story that takes only a few sentences of summary: We reached an impasse in our relationship. I recently came out to myself and to my spouse, and we are choosing to part ways. It's hard, but we are managing through to a new life. In my own experience of disclosing to friends and family, the most common response was, "I am sorry you are going through this, but I am so happy and hopeful for you as well!" Those responses were so comforting and so unexpected.

In the therapy group that I run, when a new member starts, I have each existing member share the synopsis of their story and then ask the new member to share his. The people who are further down the road inevitably have a short but complete story to tell, while those who are newer need more time and detail as they are making sense of everything. When work is done to fully understand personal circum-stances, a new, direct, and simple narrative develops that serves as the template for further disclosures. At some point, this information starts to be shared by others in the outer rings, and it spreads without any further need to personally share.

What to Say at Work

Another arena of life where people struggle with disclosure is at work, regardless of when a person comes out in their life. A 2018 study from the Human Rights Campaign determined that around forty-six percent of LGBTQ+ people in the United States choose not to disclose at their workplace. The reasons people choose to keep this part of their lives private at work run the gamut, and some can feel more amplified when coming out later in life. One reason many people for many years have stayed silent in the workplace is for fear of losing their job. I am writing this book as the United States Supreme Court recently ruled that job protections related to sex extend to sexual and gender identities. This decision is monumental and sweeping in that it is now against federal law to fire someone because they are gay or transgender. While extending federal protection is a huge step forward in LGBTQ+ rights, shedding the fear of such reprisal will take time to lessen. That is not to say that some employers may not suddenly find other performance issues to highlight, so job risk still remains.

Many people choose to keep their private life and personal life separate to a great extent, regardless of sexual identity. For many others, though, they spend a significant amount of time with coworkers and develop a sense of community where knowing more about each other deepens work bonds and overall productivity. One can usually intuit whether a work environment is safe by noting whether there are any other out people in the workplace or by looking through company policies and practices related to LGBTQ+ issues. Just as rights have expanded in many societies, so has the inclusion and protection for gay employees. That is not always the case, however, and some environments may either openly or subtly discriminate or create an environment that is unwelcoming.

Jobs are the foundation for financial security, so making the decision to come out at work can be complicated, and there is no right answer for every person in every situation. I have worked with clients who work in historically hetero-centric fields where jokes or bullying of gay people is common, and some clients have been targeted for "performance issues" that never existed before coming out. The decision to remain in the closet at work is personal and very heavy, but sometimes it is the only option in certain circumstances. It is also not uncommon for someone coming out to consider changing jobs to leave what may be a hostile work environment. Many companies, large and small, proudly communicate that they celebrate having a very diverse workforce. It is very easy to research companies with a welcoming culture, so the idea of leaving or losing a job can also become an opportunity to make professional life more rewarding. Finally, contacting a company's human resource department for advice and connection to any affinity groups that may exist in the company can be very beneficial.

If all indications are that one's workplace is welcoming and affirming to gay people, the person who comes out later also fears that their professional skills and judgment may be seen as questionable if they share that they are gay and leaving their straight marriage. That fear is usually still rooted in some shame about sexuality and choices made throughout life rather than a probable response. Just like with friends, coworkers who really know a person will understand that coming out is a tough transition and will only hope for happiness and success for their coworker.

One of the questions people usually have is about how to come out at work, and again, the options are many. Some may tell a supervisor or trusted team member first and then decide who, if anyone else, needs to know. The workplace is the perfect environment to use humor to reveal this change, and having some prepared responses is a good thing. If a coworker says that they have someone they think would be a perfect match, it is okay to simply say, "Really? What's his name?" or "Thanks, but I don't bat for that team anymore." These are gentle ways of coming out that tend to take it out of the "serious" arena and into a simple conversation that does not need or require a long or detailed conversation. One client simply changed the watch face on his smartwatch to have a rainbow background, which was a subtle and comfortable step for him.

The pattern I have more commonly seen is that a person who is coming out later and making so many adjustments in their lives is more likely to cross the bridge at work when they feel more comfortable and confident in their personal life. Some choose not to make it an issue until they have a new romantic partner in their lives and have to deal with things like office holiday parties or invitations to dinner with coworkers and their spouses. Ultimately, there is no right or wrong when it comes to workplace decisions, but the freedom to be fully oneself in all parts of life, including work, is an aspirational goal throughout the process of coming out.

Chapter 9:
HOW WILL I EXPLAIN?

This letter is from a man who started to come out at age fifty-three and more publicly at around age sixty. He had been married to women twice before, and he fathered a daughter. He learned over the years to listen more closely to his inner voice until he was ready to name and pursue his own truth.

Dear Me,

Hello there, it's me, your inner self, that secret person. I am writing you because my intuition tells me that you are having thoughts about embarking on a journey (which will prove to be an adventurous one at that) to reveal the identity of the person that has lived inside you all of your life. Yes, I'm talking about me: the very person you became aware of in your early teen years and which you also unknowingly even earlier had a glimpse of in your childhood years—the same person for many years that you have suppressed and whose existence you have denied. Yes, I'm referring to him—me.

I realize that the mere thought of revealing your most inner secret—your same-gender attraction—to not only yourself but also possibly, just maybe, to your family, friends, work colleagues and who knows who else—very much frightens and scares you. Outwardly, you have lived your life, all fifty-three years, as a straight man. And although you haven't had any uncontrollable male attraction struggles along your heterosexual path, you have all the while known (whether subconsciously or actively repressing) about the awareness of your male attraction interest. After having had two heterosexual marriages (one being eight years and the other being twelve years), the birth and raising of your daughter, and multiple heterosexual relationships, I know that you have very real fears and concerns (at least what now seem to be very real) as to what everyone will think after they know, and how they will interact with you after knowing. Will your friends and family continue loving you? Will your work colleagues (the one place where you are most private about yourself as to all aspects of your life) ostracize you? To put it simply, will you be accepted? And, ultimately, will you care if they don't?

I wish I could tell you all the details as to exactly how your coming-out journey will play out, but, unfortunately, I cannot. Everyone's coming-out journey is different. While some guys make up their mind to just do it, make a loud-speaker announcement of sorts and then get on with their new gay lifestyles, other guys "tiptoe through the tulips" along the way until they feel comfortable writing the next chapter of the journey. I know you very well and the comfort you find in creating a process for most everything you do (both personally and career-wise). My guess is that you will be a tip-toer, which is perfectly fine.

So, since you are undeniably aware of me—that inner secret person who has pulled your attention more and more over the years away from female attraction to male attraction—and because you do actually want to come out, my thoughts are for you to first acknowledge and accept ME. Your acknowledgment and acceptance of ME will be the greatest gift you can ever give yourself. That gift will provide you with the confidence, strength, and courage you will need all along the way and, most importantly, will need as you present yourself to others as the gay man that you are. And, then, once you yourself become comfortable being gay, your true authentic self, the rest of the journey—and life—will be more rewarding, more freeing, and more fun than you could ever imagine!

Now, I suspect that you might be thinking and questioning: "How do I go about doing all that? How do I become him when all I know is the comfort of being me—that secret guy living inside the box as a straight man? Where and how will I start presenting myself as a gay man? How will I make gay friends? How will I explain to my heterosexual friends that I am gay?" I'm sure that the thoughts and questions go on and on.

Well, all I can say is that I do not know exactly how your journey will play out or how long it will take, what your highs, lows, joys, disappointments, missteps and corrections, and fun times will be along the way, or what acquaintances, friendships, relationships you will experience, which relationships will become lasting or which will end abruptly, but one thing that I am sure of is that you, in the end, will thrive and that the unwrapping of you in the process of your coming out will be adventurous, fun, and SO MUCH WORTH IT!

I am confident that you will grow and strengthen in many ways as you walk across the coming-out bridge toward that colorful rainbow that awaits and represents you and your new open lifestyle. And I can tell you that, as you get closer and closer to that rainbow, you will see the colors start to have special meaning and ultimately energize you like a breath of fresh mountain air!

So, for now, I want to leave you with this: please remember that your worst nightmare thoughts about coming out will have no resemblance to reality. Trust me! I look forward to walking with you!

Chapter 10:
TO CHANGE OR END A MARRIAGE

The word divorce conjures up so many negative thoughts and feelings that contemplating this step may seem unthinkable. The language around divorce is often apocalyptic: broken family, destroyed lives, complete failure. Some equate it with financial ruin and abandonment of responsibility. The reality is that many marriages end in divorce for many reasons. Technically and legally, a divorce is simply the end of a marital contract between two people. In the real world, it means so much more than that. A divorce can be the absolute best choice for a struggling and dysfunctional couple in some cases. That does not make it easy for anyone, but it may be a needed resolution that deflates the tension and unhappiness that are causing more damage than the divorce ever will.

People often look with wonder as to why two people stay married when they are clearly unhappy, unsatisfied, or lacking in the necessary love and communication to keep a relationship alive and healthy. Some stick it out for the kids, and others hold religious beliefs that a marriage commitment is for life, no matter what. Clearly, marriages that include domestic abuse, whether physical, sexual, verbal, emotional, or otherwise, have stakes that are very high and urgent that defy even the most strongly held moral position. In any event, contemplating the decision to divorce or not is complicated and an emotional landmine. Divorce takes time and can be approached in several ways to minimize the emotional and financial toll on all parties.

Mixed Orientation Marriages

Does coming out later automatically result in divorce? The answer is usually yes but not always and not always quickly. Some couples explore options to see if maintaining a marriage may be viable, but both need to be honest about wanting to try. If either party is walking down that lane only to appease their partner and turn down the chaos, their efforts will usually be in vain. I worked with individuals and couples who remained in a "mixed-orientation marriage." The reality is they were always in a mixed-orientation marriage; it is just now being recognized, explored, and named. Couples make this decision based on many factors. Perhaps they both feel that most of their needs are well met by the relationship, and sex is not that important to either of them. Sometimes the idea of "breaking up" a family with children is not what they deem best for anyone. Another force to stay together is financial, and the perceived cost would be practically too much. Regardless of the reasoning, both parties choose to move forward with full knowledge that one partner's sexual attractions lie primarily outside of the marriage.

Some decide to open the sexual or emotional boundaries on both sides of the relationship. Others work to recommit to monogamy while being honest and open about the struggles and fears along the way. It takes time to live with either of these realities and experience their impact on the relationship. Some believe that it will be manageable, only to learn in practice that it is much harder than they hoped it would be. Having a marriage survive requires redefining the relationship to something new, which often comes with mourning the loss of what was. That transition takes time, effort, care, and above all, honesty. Even with the best of intentions and very hard work, that new relationship may not be the relationship either really wants or feels they deserve. If a couple is considering this path, seeking help and support from competent professionals or experienced support networks is a must.

Divorce and Its Aftermath

If divorce is the more likely outcome, several aspects must be understood from the beginning. Divorce is inherently a legal process that takes time and costs money. Some divorces can happen relatively quickly, in two to three months, but they generally take somewhat longer. If contested and taken to court, the process can last years and become incredibly expensive. Many options exist for couples to create a process that feels as fair and respectful as possible, preserves and protects children, and avoids some of the steep financial pitfalls. I am not a lawyer, and I cannot offer legal advice of any kind. Laws vary from state to state and sometimes from jurisdiction to jurisdiction. It is important to research local divorce law, talk with others who have been through a divorce, and consult with attorneys and divorce mediators. I can share some lessons learned from what I observed with clients and in my own divorce.

The most typical scenario involves both parties hiring a lawyer who, often with a mediator, facilitates agreements about finances and custody that will make up the final divorce paperwork. The agreements need to be very detailed and can be complicated depending on the overall family and financial picture. One thing to be prepared to accept is that neither party ever leaves the mediation process feeling like they got everything they wanted. Compromise is part of the solution, and the more flexibility in that arena, the quicker and less expensive it will be. If the family has significant wealth and assets, the financial agreements can take a long time, as financial experts generally need to be involved. Contested custody proceedings also can take a very long time as psychological and home evaluations must take place. The days of lifetime alimony are mostly gone, and child support and custody arrangements usually apply until a child turns eighteen or graduates from high school. Spousal support most commonly ends early if that spouse remarries. Divorce law is ever evolving and changing, however, and seeking the guidance of professionals is essential and well worth the investment.

Collaborative divorce is a helpful approach many couples take, which usually involves a commitment to keep the proceeding from ever reaching a trial and letting disagreements be resolved through mediation. Collaborative divorce involves lawyers, financial planners or CPAs, and childcare mental health specialists, all trained in the collaborative process. This team helps minimize the emotional toll and lowers the costs related to divorce. Some mediation groups also exist that can work with couples to reach a mutual agreement before lawyers get involved. Some couples who approach divorce from an amicable place can sometimes work out the details of what they want themselves to be presented to a lawyer for preparation, which is usually the least expensive option. Divorces run anywhere from a few thousand dollars to tens of thousands of dollars and much more if disputes end up in court. When faced with that reality, many couples do understandably seek to limit the financial burden of the divorce itself.

Ultimately, both parties sign a written agreement related to finances and custody, which is then submitted to a judge. In the state of Georgia, where I live and practice, a thirty-day waiting period exists once that paperwork is filed, but the judge can simply sign off on the agreement any time after that. One's lawyer simply calls and informs their client that the divorce is final. Some states also require education for the divorcing parties about how to manage the process when children are involved. These sessions need to be completed before paperwork submission, and they are more informative and helpful than most usually expect.

The idea that the divorce will leave someone penniless and homeless is baseless, but some change to the standard of living is a very real adjustment that often follows. That change is quickly offset by the ability to freely move on and create a new life that is honest and in alignment with self. The value of completing the divorce can't be experienced until it is finished, but that value often outweighs the costs in ways that are truly rewarding and meaningful.

My former wife and I chose to attend our divorce proceeding together. In what I think was surprising to the judge, we held hands as the divorce decree was signed. We had both been feeling such stress as the day approached, and we decided to support each other in that moment. For us, there was something poetic in standing together just as we did the day the marriage began. Afterward, I accompanied her to furniture stores as she chose new bedroom furniture for herself. The day of the divorce coincided with one of the largest torrential downfalls we had ever seen in Atlanta with flooding around the city. Much to the furniture salesperson's delight, we were trapped in the store for hours during the storm. We kept adding more items as time wore on. Needless to say, the day was memorable in many bittersweet ways.

The emotional ups and downs of the divorce process and its aftermath are understandably significant. Ending a marriage is a huge change to identity and family, and if it were easy or enjoyable, that would be a much greater cause for concern. Walking around a house full of memories and memorabilia with an eye on division can be overwhelming at first. Realizing that the retirement nest egg divided by two does not go as far is unnerving and stressful. Trying to determine where a child may spend holidays and summers in the future may feel cruel and unfair. Approaching these tasks gets easier each time an attempt is made, and they do get completed. Some deep disagreements may surface that are ultimately decided by a mediator or judge, and their decision could be hard to swallow and feel punitive. Once the process is complete and the agreement is final, at least both parties can begin to move forward and plan their future with concrete information about finances, etc.

The day comes when the divorce is officially complete, and so begins what I call "The Year of Firsts." The first holidays, birthdays, anniversaries, and family rituals under this new structure come to pass. Each of those days may seem daunting, especially if they are spent alone. I spent the first Thanksgiving following my divorce alone.

I enjoyed driving around Atlanta without traffic, and I took in some good movies and Chinese food. I also wept often and uncontrollably at times. The year of firsts is incredibly hard, but it is survivable. It also becomes easier with each event and with the passage of time. A new normal sets in with new rewards and new rituals, either independently or with family. With each passing day, a greater sense of self and direction lays the foundation for hope and joy to return.

The last subject about the aftermath of divorce is new primary relationships developing for both parties. As those grow and deepen, the boundaries established after the divorce may need some tweaking or stretching. The reality is also that both parties get to choose for themselves who they date and introduce into their family system, and their former spouse may not be jumping up and down with joy about their choice. Absent any real and measurable threat to any children involved, respect must be afforded regarding these choices. After a divorce, you no longer have a say in most personal decisions your former spouse makes, and the need to treat others as you wish to be treated is paramount.

Chapter 11:
BEING AN OUT PARENT

Many men who come out later in life had children if they were first married to a woman. Fear of the impact coming out could have on kids played a part in avoiding the issue of sexuality. Even after coming out, some retain a fear that they have somehow damaged their children irrevocably, regardless of their children's reactions. Learning to make peace with those fears and learning to be an out parent have their own learning curve.

Impacts on Children

Have I worked with any clients whose children had a negative reaction or outright rejected them? Yes, I have. It is the exception by far, and in every situation that I have seen, those children were already adults. As described earlier, adult children often react similarly to straight spouses with deep anger and suspicion about whether anything was ever true. Healing those divides is not easy or quick. If the divorce was highly contentious, they might also feel a need to stay in the role of protector to the aggrieved spouse recovering from the upheaval in the family. The best prescription is to be patient, available, and honest in communication and interaction. Adult children will need time to rebuild trust one step at a time.

Regardless of the age of children when coming out happens, there are ways to approach the changes with parenting as a focus. A parent can role model important life lessons about facing adversity with dignity, being accountable for mistakes, and telling the truth no matter how hard it is. A child may be relieved to know that their parent is not perfect, and so they don't have to be perfect. Additionally, when the buffer from being in the closet disappears, one gets the opportunity to develop an even deeper personal relationship with children.

Fortunately, the world today has more and more positive examples of gay people and gay relationships. Younger people and teens feel much more at ease expressing and exploring sexual variations for themselves and accepting them in their friends. While one may have thought having a gay parent would be a curse for a child, the reality is that, in some ways, it is kind of cool now. At the very least, the story of a parent coming out makes great material for college admission essays! Not to make too light of this situation, just trust that being an out parent is not dipped in the shame and embarrassment that we may have experienced years ago. As in most relational situations, the most important tactic is to keep lines of communication open. Teach your children how to talk about it when you need to, and then give them space to talk about it when they need to.

Introducing Children to Friends and Partners

One question that eventually presents itself is when to introduce children to gay friends and romantic interests. The approach is very different for each. As a new circle of gay friends develops, do not be shy about introducing children to them. If they are good and trustworthy people, it will do children good to see that their parent is doing well and supported by friends. If friends are kept out of sight, the child will receive subtle shame messages about gay friends and about being gay at all. Being honest and open with them means they will feel safer and more comfortable in general. Exposure to friends also will make the eventual introduction of a romantic interest feel more natural.

The decision to introduce your children to boyfriends or partners depends on the age of the children, the level of support they feel from both parents, and a parent's personal comfort level with being in a same-sex relationship. For younger children, introducing someone too soon is likely not beneficial. They need predictability in their routines and surroundings, and introducing people that could soon disappear is not necessary. If a relationship has progressed from dating to a true commitment, then letting the children meet him is a natural step forward in the relationship. One important aspect to keep in mind is that this decision should be made no differently than if introducing an opposite-sex relationship. All divorced parents have to learn the ropes with dating again, and it is important to not overweight the scales on any decision because it is a same-sex relationship. That would again subtly indicate that same-sex relationships are somehow more scary or shameful.

One man I know developed a committed relationship with another man after being married to a woman for a couple of decades. When the time came to introduce his new partner to his son, he first partnered with his former wife to set the conditions for the introduction. His son, who was a young teenager at that point, was hesitant at first. After some time, he expressed a willingness to meet with one condition: he wanted to meet the new partner one-on-one. The parents and the new partner were taken aback at first about such a request but honored what he wanted. During that initial meeting, the new partner asked the son why he wanted to meet with just the two of them. The son stated simply, "I just think it's easier to get to know someone one-on-one." While the grown-ups had a lot of anxiety about this initial encounter, the son had a truly grown-up and open intention.

Another consideration when raising children as an out parent is to seek out other gay parents with similarly aged children. Some cities have play groups for gay parents and their children. These connections help children know that they are not the only ones out there with a gay dad, and it can help normalize the new family structure, not to mention parent and child alike may make some good new friends as well. These groups also become a good resource to learn how other parents approach a wide variety of situations, including schools, families, and friends.

The last topic regarding parenting is that as children become adults with their own new relationships, they may have additional questions or issues with the changes that result from a parent coming out. Perhaps a divorce had a greater impact than they could see at the time. Perhaps they have a new understanding of how hard any relationship can be as they go through their own inevitable heartbreaks.

My son has always been incredibly loving and supportive of my identity since he learned about it in middle school. The subsequent divorce and change in circumstances had their impacts on him, but we tried to keep lines of communication always open and honest. When he started engaging in adult relationships of his own, he realized that he played caretaker to me when growing up, which started to show up in unhealthy ways in his own relationships. He bravely looked at himself and also held me to account for my part in this pattern ten years after I came out. Revisiting that time in both our lives was another opportunity to role model honesty, accountability, and acceptance. I tried my best to listen with understanding, respond with truth, apologize for some mistakes I made, and let him know that I love him deeply.

Chapter 12:
RESOLVING
FAITH CONFLICTS

Men raised in a specific faith tradition who come out later in life have a host of ideas about the place they want religion, faith, or spirituality to have in their lives. Some had an overall positive experience in their faith history and fear that coming out will cost them access to that resource of support. Others heard ongoing negative messages about who they are that left deep wounds and anger, so leaving the religious world behind becomes a welcomed relief when coming out. Regardless of where a person's experience lies in that spectrum, some resolution is likely needed to either reconnect to faith or to release the anger and resentment induced by faith.

What Do I Believe?

Being gay and being religious or spiritual are not by any means polar opposites. Those who grew up in a faith tradition that held very rigid beliefs about the sinfulness of homosexuality may find that hard to believe. They likely were taught that anyone who tried to claim that homosexuality was not sinful or an abomination was doing the work of Satan. Considering the possibility that what was taught in religious settings may not be true can be a big step to take.

I do not pretend to be a religious expert of any kind, nor am I fluent in the vast array of religious beliefs and teachings across all the great religions of the world. I was personally raised in the Catholic Church, but I sought other denominations in adulthood when I found difficulty reconciling several of my personal beliefs with the specific teachings of the church. When I stepped into alternative worship settings and denominations, the experience did not feel like church to me at first. As I grew to know more people and become familiar with different worship styles, what was new and at odds with all I had been taught became familiar and a new experience of church that felt real and true. These changes happened before I came out and had to cross that theological bridge. I had already begun examining what I truly believed when it came to faith and religion. My point here is that when something is new and feels at odds with what was familiar, it may evolve into something that feels even better.

In order to begin resolving faith conflicts internally, one must first examine what they really believe and if they want to have a specific faith identity. Church and faith communities may have been part of the closet and perhaps never truly resonated. On the other hand, being part of a faith community and its support may have been one of the most valued aspects of life, and the feared potential loss of that resource felt immense. This transition time can be an opportunity to explore many different faith practices and beliefs to see if anything feels more in alignment with personal beliefs and values.

Healing Religious Trauma

What steps are necessary to resolve faith conflicts and historical wounds? The answers are different for different people. We will begin with those who feel sorely traumatized by religion and now identify as agnostic or atheist with no desire to engage faith communities. Anyone who experiences any form of trauma will need some help in releasing themselves from the carnage so that they can live a life free from anger and resentment about what came before. A growing field of specialty within the mental health community is the area of religious trauma. The process involves creating a sense of security and safety in one's current environment, where the threat of repeating the trauma is low. With that sense of security, one can fully explore the details of what happened and what lingers, as well as search for the meaningful lessons that can be taken forward. The final step is to learn to reconnect in the world without the past hurts claiming hold of the heart or mind. It is not a fast or painless journey but one well worth taking with the help of qualified and competent professionals.

Some people in this transition discover that they no longer hold any specific religious beliefs, whether they identify as atheist or agnostic. Either religion never played much of a role in their life before, or they assess that they participated simply out of an effort to keep closeted. Depending on beliefs held by family and friends, stepping out of faith practices may lead to additional alienation at first, but most understand that faith communities may no longer feel safe to someone who is out.

We will next examine what steps a person may take if they want to reconnect to a previous faith practice or seek out a new one. The best place to begin is by searching out writings or talks from people within a faith tradition that have an open and affirming stance.

Resources exist online for gay Christians, Jews, and Muslims, which can be found in the appendix. Great people of great faith within these communities have worked to bridge the perceived gaps between faith and sexuality. Depending on where one lives, there may be churches, synagogues, or mosques nearby that are open and affirming. Whether through online or live resources, using the work others have done before can be incredibly helpful.

Finding Safe Faith Communities

If able to access local churches and faith communities, research should be done about where each may fully stand. Often a church's website may not make any reference to its stance on sexuality and communicate an openness to anyone who would want to attend. These churches are honestly the places that require the most thorough investigation. I describe churches in three ways: not open or affirming, open but not affirming, and open and affirming. Churches that are not open and affirming are usually pretty easy to spot. Their online information usually includes a commitment to heteronormative values such as the sanctity of the male/female relationship. They often have writings or stories online readily available that support their belief. I do not fault these churches for being upfront about their opposition to supporting gay people. In fact, I appreciate it. Churches that are open and affirming, on the other hand, usually also prominently make that known on their website and in their literature. They often include LGBTQ+ ministries and organizations, and perhaps some of their clergy or administration identify as members of the LGBTQ+ community.

The churches that are open but not affirming are usually the ones that make that distinction hard to pin down. They often have a very open and welcoming worship style and community, and they play down any controversy around LGBTQ+ issues. They are happy to have members of the community worship with them, serve in some capacities, and donate to their mission. Upon closer look, however, none of the leadership identifies as LGBTQ+, or if they do, they have publicly committed to a life of celibacy. If you are attending a new church and you are unsure about where they stand, simply talk with someone on the pastoral staff and ask if an openly gay person in a committed and loving relationship can serve in the education ministry and work with children. If the answer is no (we must protect the children), then you will know that they are open and not affirming.

Gay people returning to church need to make sure they are in a safe and welcoming space to reconnect to their spiritual life. Sometimes, it is best to start in a church setting that is more exclusively gay in population to assure that safety. An exclusively gay church may or may not become a permanent home, but it can serve as a bridge back to worship and a faith community. The first time I sat in a church with openly LGBTQ+ members singing and worshiping right there with everyone else, I cried, and my own faith wounds began to heal.

Chapter 13:
IDENTITY EXPLORATION AND DEVELOPMENT

There is a wealth of research about how identity development works for all people, as well as identity development specific to topics like sexual identity. I am not a huge fan of linear developmental models that prescribe the order of what you will feel, indicating a clear finish line ahead. One usually bounces between stages or may be in multiple stages simultaneously. Considering the different stages, however, can be helpful as a guide to the personal journey of coming out.

Sexual Identity Development Models

The original researched model for sexual identity development is the Cass Identity Model, created in 1979 by Vivienne Cass for the Journal of Homosexuality. The named stages were:

➤ Identity Confusion

➤ Identity Comparison

➤ Identity Tolerance

➤ Identity Acceptance

➤ Identity Pride

➤ Identity Synthesis

Many other researchers have refined these concepts to address different experiences related to various sexual identities and experiences, such as socio-economic factors, the evolving impact of social stigma, and the incorrect assumption that not completing each stage leads to maladjustment. Once again, all these models are based on research that tries to describe the general experience of coming into acceptance and authenticity with sexual identity. In a general themed overview, the stages follow a similar pattern: feeling unsure and confused about personal identity, taking steps to understand self and others with varying identities, working to accept and then even celebrate this aspect of self, and finally balancing sexual identity with all other parts of identity. These same stages can be applied to the development of many aspects of identity: gender experience, racial identity, faith beliefs, and professional development. One unique nuance of coming out later in life is that many aspects of identity went through predictable stages of development, while sexual identity was left behind to a certain extent.

Clients who sit on my couch and can say that they are gay are already resolving the identity confusion stage. The next stages of identity comparison, exploration, and acceptance are part of the early work in coming out. A couple of tasks related to each stage can help with overall growth: immersion and advocacy. While these tasks do not need to wait until one is fully out, they are often more fully experienced and powerful when one can be free to openly express this aspect of self.

Immersion

Immersion is not about diving headfirst into the deep end of the gay pool, which can be pretty dangerous if you don't know how to swim in that pool. It does mean exposure to gay-friendly and inclusive environments. One piece of homework I assign clients is to spend time in places where one doesn't have to come out because the specific environmental presumption is that one is gay. Depending on where you live, this assignment may be easy or very hard. In Atlanta, like many metropolitan areas, there are specific neighborhoods, shopping centers, and, of course, bars and clubs that cater specifically to the gay community. If someone has never had any exposure, I usually ask them to spend some time in a coffee shop where most of the patrons are gay. Such experience allows being seen by others who expect that you are gay without the pressure of interacting at first. It also allows observation of gay people in their many, many forms that will challenge any stereotypical beliefs about what being gay looks like. Choosing to attend events or joining social groups that cater to the LBGTQ+ community is a next step that gives a peek into this new community. Stepping into a gay bar or the like for the first time can be pretty nerve-racking, especially if going alone. Sometimes, it is better to do the work of making new friends in the community first who can help give an overview of what to expect in different settings.

When one of my former clients reported feeling ready to expand his level of exposure, he wanted to step into a gay bar for the first time. I suggested a local gay sports bar (yes, they exist!). This bar was truly a friendly, sports-oriented bar with many patrons who were more of my client's age and background. I believed this environment would line up best with my client's interests and personality, resulting in a more comfortable exposure. He bravely followed through and quickly shared that he was very uncomfortable and could not imagine ever going back. As with any exposure to something new, consistency and repetition develop comfort. After returning several times in the following weeks, he shared that he had found his place and his people. Patrons and bartenders knew his name and story, and he developed many friends that remain close to this day.

For those who live in a smaller town or more rural area, opportunities like these may not be accessible. Even if they are possible, the first exposure in public may seem like a step too far at first. A place to begin is through reading books and articles or watching movies, documentaries, and TV shows with an LGBTQ+ focus (see recommendations in the appendix). Various online support groups exist for men who are or were married to women, such as how-support.org for husbands out or coming out to wives. Spending time exploring online resources can be a way to feel connected.

Planning a weekend getaway to a city with a thriving gay community is another way to gain exposure. Much like Airbnb, the site Misterb&b offers short-term housing opportunities offered to gay men. The site also includes guides to cities and what activities or outings may be good. Another resource is the GayCities website. A search of GayCities with a specific city name will render a list of hotels, restaurants, bars, clubs, and events that cater to the LGBTQ+ community. The main idea is to explore a world that includes people who are happy, feeling true peace and connection in life, and who also happen to be gay. Seeking tangible examples of what is possible on the other side of coming out can be a salve to the anxiety and fear about what the future may hold.

For those who pursued sex with other men before coming out, those experiences can create an extremely narrow and wholly incomplete vision of what being out is like. Those sexual experiences happen with the goal of staying hidden, so all kinds of negative projections arise about self and all gay men. These encounters usually result in wanting to stay in the closet even more. Limited sexual interactions are tenuous at best and support the faulty belief that gay men are incapable of healthy and complete relationships, are sexually reckless, and have lives equally as unfulfilled as those in the closet. Without affirming experiences that show the possibility that safety and contentment are real and possible, one can remain convinced that only utter destruction awaits.

Advocacy

Another task related to identity exploration and development is advocacy. When a person hears the word advocacy, many hear a call to become a public advocate for gay issues. Many organizations work very hard every day to pursue, protect, and promote the rights of gay people all over the world. Their tireless devotion has reaped the rewards and saved many lives, and volunteering for those causes in small and big ways is a fantastic form of advocacy. Early in the process of coming out, however, it can seem way too daunting. Even when fully out and comfortable, that kind of work may not be in your wheelhouse. In the early stages of coming out, advocacy includes every step one takes. Stating your truth publicly for the first time is advocacy. Trying to better understand yourself and seek truth is advocacy. Being a patron at a gay-owned business is advocacy.

I had a client whose child attended a private, Christian school that was not affirming of homosexuality or gay relationships. Early in his work with me, he expressed fears of what it would be like to go to his child's high school graduation if he were out. What if he had a partner or husband by then and the two of them were sitting in the audience and everybody knew they were a couple? While statistics about how many gay people exist are hard to pin down and controversial, common sense tells us that in a group of graduating high school seniors, there are bound to be a few gay people. If in an environment that teaches that being gay is wrong and harmful, most likely any young gay person is deeply hiding their truth in such a school. Imagine that young person looking into the families at their graduation and seeing a gay couple, happy and proud as can be. Seeing them, at that moment, could save a young life. Now that is some very important advocacy that one might not foresee or even know is happening. By the way, that same client did find himself sitting at his child's high school graduation with his husband, and it was a day of great pride for father and child alike.

Through activities related to immersion and advocacy, a person can start to develop comfort with being out and better understand the possibilities that are available when out. This exploration is about figuring out the best environments that line up with a person's interests and values. Spending time in various gay environments does not mean making some kind of commitment to a lifestyle. Seeing various gay bars or going to gay-oriented get-togethers is about learning what is available and what fits and then making more informed choices from there about how to socialize and build friendships with people who have similar interests.

Chapter 14:
THIS IS YOUR LIFE

T he following letter was written by a man who came out at age forty-five after seventeen years of marriage and fathering one son. Like many, he had to sift through the hurts of the past to start to discover who he really was and to claim his own path to true happiness.

Dear Me,

You have just taken a huge step in your life of authenticity and your belief in yourself. Listen to me when I tell you about the amount of courage it took to begin a journey of finding and being yourself. When I say courage, I know you may struggle with that. Yes, you broke free of being stuck, and that is courage. Your journey of learning about yourself is beginning. There is a lot of work that you will need to put in. You will need to sort out your past and your future. This will involve being open and honest and investing in yourself. Getting a qualified therapist will be a great value, as well as belonging to a peer group going through the same as you. You need help on this journey, and it should be from unbiased persons. Be as open and honest with these people about things that may come up from the past, current, and future. Talking about it and sorting through all of your story will help to begin the life that you thought would never happen.

I know it is hard to tell your wife, family, friends, and your son. You worry about what they will think and how they will feel about you. All the people you have told are the ones who love you, and your sexual orientation does not change that. Coming out is news for them, and it will take some getting accustomed to. You have worked hard to keep and maintain these relationships and even supported them in some of their life ups and downs. It will take time, but if you remain positive, your support network will be supportive of you. Just keep in mind you are learning about yourself now. Things will be different. Don't assume other people's thoughts, and don't write a story of something that you think might be true. Validate your thoughts and be mindful that your feelings are true. Also, stop comparing yourself to other people. Take ownership of how you feel and how your thinking tells a story of truth. All your life, you have lived to please others and seek approval. Look in the mirror and put that stamp of approval on yourself and live for you.

You are extremely close with your son. One of your happiest days is his entry into this world. You take pride in being a good father. You are a parent who has been there for him, raising him to be a great man. Your gift to him is what your dad could not give you. Telling him will be hard, and it will take patience to let him figure it out. Answer his questions and teach him about your new community. Let him know you are still the same Dad—

nothing is different. Yes, you told him you were gay, and now Mom and Dad are getting a divorce. Work with your former wife to support him. She will need to figure things out, and that will take time, too. You are not responsible for her choices. You may not agree with all the things she does with your son, and that is okay.

Focus on yourself and learn to love yourself. As the famous RuPaul says, "If you can't love yourself, how the hell you gonna love somebody else." Again, invest in yourself and go through all the "monsters" from your past that have shaped you and the voices in your head. Put those "monsters" in a place where you can visualize them for what they truly are. These "monsters" are beliefs that you own and hold, so take the time to analyze them and set them free. Break them down piece by piece until you understand the reality of the "monsters." Moving forward, I want you to remember three questions when faced with adversity and worries. Is it real? Is it me? Is it today? These are good questions to validate and process thoughts. This is mindful thinking and not jumping to conclusions.

Once you are comfortable with loving yourself, put yourself out there to find that soul mate that you have wanted and dreamed of. It will be hard. You will meet a lot of great people and not-so-great people. Remember that not everybody wants the same thing in life that you do. It will take practice. Think of it as going through your adolescent years again. Also, be mindful not to paint broad strokes about the gay community. The community is like the straight community, meaning there are many ways people identify themselves. Set those boundaries for those you meet. Be open and honest because you are protecting the new you that you are building. No one is perfect, but you need to know that it takes work for a relationship to thrive. The more communication and compromise, the better life will be. In all your relationships, express how you are feeling about things that may come up. Don't put the ownership immediately on the person you feel your troubles are with. Speak to them about how you feel. Also, keep in mind that it is not always about you. What problems and troubles does that person have? Ask them and let them know you are there to listen because you value them.

This is your life—claim and own it. There will be tears, and there will be pain, but it's what you do with the pain that matters. Don't set timelines for when you think things will be better. Also, know the path and journey will have many ups and downs. Recognize the ups and downs and learn and grow from them. You truly are worthy, and life is beginning. Don't waste a moment of this wonderful life you have been gifted.

I love you, and your determination and dedication are in you!

Section Three:
BEING OUT

Chapter 15:
SINGLE LIFE AND THE WORLD OF DATING

Building a new life as a single person is daunting enough. Learning to adapt to life as a gay man in a community that may seem somewhat foreign and new makes it all the more complicated. For those who never married but remained closeted, the experience of being single and open about their sexuality is also novel. This road is filled with twists and turns that can be intimidating and confusing. We will explore many facets to consider with some recommendations about how to navigate this new world while holding onto all of who you are as well. Understanding readiness to date is imperative. Gaining some insight into the language, varied subgroups, and relationship options that gay men practice is helpful. Having some guidance about where and how dating happens—online and offline—can make maneuvering this world a bit less stressful. Lastly, education about dating and sexual health in today's world can open up incredible possibilities that may be dismissed or overlooked.

Single Again

On the other side of coming out to family and friends, as well as making any subsequent changes to family structure, is the experience of being out and single. For those who did marry, it may be many years since being single and engaging in the world of dating. No more having to say, "I'm going through a divorce," which is always fraught with questions and unknown timelines. You can simply state, "I am divorced." Being single includes learning to live and make decisions for and by yourself. The idea of setting up a home or apartment that can reflect your taste can be exciting. Making decisions about what to eat, what to wear, and how to spend free time without clearing it with anyone else is also pretty freeing.

Learning to live and spend time alone without having to feel lonely is often the difficult part at first. This alone time is an opportunity to devote some effort to interests that you and your spouse may not have shared. If outdoor adventuring, whether kayaking, mountain biking, or hiking, was something you enjoyed solo, now is the time to join some group activities around these pursuits. Perhaps a reading club or board game group would be a fun new alternative. Even better would be to find gay groups that engage in these activities. These types of social engagement will increase the number of new friends, as well as keep the newly cleared calendar somewhat booked. Meetup.com is a website devoted to connecting people with similar interests. In most metropolitan areas, one can search any activity, add the word gay, and social groups built around that activity will pop up. Not all friends and activities must be with other gay people, but the greater the exposure, the greater the resulting comfort level with this new community. Eventually, you will start to form a network of friends that only know you as a gay man, which becomes very comforting.

Am I Available?

I am out and single, but am I ready and fully available? Sometimes, when you come out and matriculate through this process, you immediately want to find a new, committed, loving relationship with a man. While wanting that is understandable, it is the "immediately" part that needs some tending to when entering the world of dating. I ask clients to first assess what they are truly available for. If they are still grieving the loss of what was, they likely are not fully available for a relationship with someone new. If they are still harboring some aspects of internalized homophobia, they likely are not fully available for a relationship. They may be ready to meet people and explore their sexuality, but being available for a true commitment may be down the line a bit. So, how do you know when you are truly available? Being available becomes apparent as certain milestones are achieved:

> You know and understand your own values about relationships and sex.
> You are free and comfortable expressing your emotional and sexual intimacy with another man.
> You are comfortable introducing a partner to family and friends.
> You realize that finding a partner with whom to share life would be great but is not required.

Engaging in the world of dating for gay men after living as straight requires some reflection on personal values. The heterosexual norms of asking a woman out, going on three dates before sex, paying for everything, and holding doors, are less defined when dating other men. Sometimes a relationship begins as a sexual hook-up that leads to greater conversation and connection. Some men like to have sex on a first date to assess if things are a good fit before deciding to open up more emotionally. Some men do prefer a more "old-fashioned" dating style and taking things slowly. It is a world with many possibilities, and anything goes. Hence it is vital to do some honest reflection on your own values to help guide the dating process. The following are some of the issues that should be explored when jumping more deeply into the dating pool:

> Are you comfortable having sex just for fun?
> Does having sex with someone equate to dating them, like it often does in the straight world?
> Are you comfortable dating or sleeping with more than one person at a time?
> What are the parameters for yourself about when something starts to move from casual to more serious?
> What are the essential things you must have in any primary relationship as opposed to things that would just be nice to have?

Second Adolescence

Another common occurrence in the out-late process is experiencing what is known as a "second adolescence." The return of feelings and behaviors that many may recall from actual physical adolescence return: insecurities about appearance, nervousness about engaging potential romantic partners, social and sexual behaviors that may be excessive, and emotional ups and downs out of proportion to actual circumstances. Many men made personal appearance choices in clothing and haircuts that conformed to looking as straight as possible. They sometimes prefer to be overweight and physically out of shape as a way of avoiding being attractive to anyone or as a way of coping with the dissonance they carried inside. Once they are single and seeking a relationship, they may explore variations in appearance that are more in alignment with their actual tastes or with what they perceive other gay men would find attractive. The transformation on the outside during the internal shift may vary for a while as one explores their own tastes and style without the constraints of having to conform to a straight appearance.

When engaging in the dating world, many people start to feel things they may have never felt before. It is not uncommon that men who come out late did not date extensively in youth, and their dating skills and tolerances are yet to be developed. Feeling extreme butterflies and anxiety about a first date and what might happen can be pretty uncomfortable at first. Spending time analyzing every word, facial expression, or physical gesture following an interaction may be totally engrossing. Great confusion about how dating works may set in, especially when it involves two men rather than the more commonly understood man/woman customs:

➤ Who pays for dinner on a date?
➤ Are there things like a "no sex until the third date" rule?
➤ If we have gone on a few dates, are we actually dating, or is it something else?

Feeling that level of self-consciousness is what is meant by a return to adolescence, which can be very strange when someone feels pretty confident in all the other arenas of adult life.

Socializing can also return to the world of adolescence. People may tend to stay out later and drink a lot more as they manage their insecurities in new environments. They may cling to new social friends intensely to feel a sense of belonging in this unfamiliar landscape. In an effort to develop new friendships and dating opportunities, they may over-commit to social activities and even overspend on outings without their more typical self-control. A pattern of engaging in frequent and irresponsible sexual practices may develop with this newfound freedom to explore sexuality more fully. Subsequent feelings of disappointment after a sexual encounter that may have meant little to their partner are also part of the emotional ups and downs that take some getting used to.

The reality is that everything a person learned about themselves over the years may feel a little off kilter for a while, but self-confidence usually returns in much less time than it took in actual adolescence. A person takes some time to learn about themselves and this new world. He is then better able to see what fits into his own sense of meaning and value, which developed throughout adulthood. Experiences that are shiny, new, scary, and exciting at first become more familiar and predictable. Returning to personally valued expectations about friendship and romance happens over time. How long that takes varies, and some notable obstacles and pitfalls show up along the way that will need monitoring and managing.

Labels and Lingo

One aspect of initiating into the gay community is being able to orient oneself within the wide expanse of gay identities, friendships, sexual practices, and relationships. For the uninitiated, there are a great many classifications by physical and behavioral types in the gay community. Learning and understanding the language around these is important while remembering that these classifications are never meant to be a complete definition of who a person is. Trouble results if a person feels like they now have to conform to some new expectation based on appearance, which is not so different from conforming to definitions of what straight appearance and behavior are.

Let's begin by diving back into one of my favorite things: definitions! Some may be new, and some may be familiar, but it is important to have a resource that helps dispel any misunderstandings. First, let's explore the various terms related to type classifications in the gay community:

> **Bear**—this is usually a physically rounder or stouter man with a beard and plenty of body hair who enjoys a good beer, a good game, and a good laugh. They are known to be incredibly friendly but tend to gravitate to their own kind in social and dating settings.
> **Cub**—a younger version of a bear
> **Wolf**—a bear that prefers to be single and avoid relationships
> **Otter**—a skinny version of a bear or cub
> **Twink**—a thin, smooth, young man with style and panache and attitude to boot
> **Twunk**—a more muscular version of a twink

> **Jock**—a clean-cut, athletic type of man who may appear
  to be straight
> **Bull**—the bodybuilder version of a jock
> **Daddy**—an older, masculine male who loves to take care of you
> **DILF**—a daddy I'd like to fuck
> **Geek**—somewhat nerdy type with a variety of passions in life

All of the above examples classify someone according to their appearance, or they are used to communicate the type of person someone finds attractive. These labels are just that—labels. They should be approached with humor and a grain of salt and not used to predict anyone's personality or character. Do some take these descriptions of physical characteristics as an absolute predictor of personality and interests? Yes, they do, which runs dangerously close to the same kind of discrimination and pigeon-holing gay people can feel from the straight community. Sometimes a newly out gay man feels more comfortable around others that fit his own physical type. If a man is forty-five, five feet tall, 200 pounds, and has a beard, he may feel self-conscious at first, surrounded by a bunch of men in their early twenties who are skinny, smooth, and full of attitude. Sometimes, finding spaces with similar types feels most comfortable, which is a good way to become oriented and feel safe within a new community.

The next definitions to examine are sexual positions:

> **Top**—a man who penetrates during sex, usually anally but also orally. Some men identify as tops exclusively, refusing to be in any other position.
> **Bottom**—a person being penetrated anally

> **Power bottom**—a bottom who likes to be in charge during sex. Some men also identify exclusively as bottoms and refuse to top. Men who enjoy both positions are referred to as
> **Versatile**—enjoying both topping and bottoming
> **Top/vers or Bottom/vers**—preferring one position but open to any
> **Side**—someone who enjoys a full range of sexual content and activities but prefers not to engage anally in any way

Sexual acts between men can be complicated from an emotional and psychological aspect, especially when first freely exploring. The sexual roles men play with each other can be infused at times with misogyny or internalized homophobia. If being a top is seen by someone as the masculine role, while being a bottom is feminine and submissive, that thought process may be in the world of ranking masculinity ahead of femininity and therefore misogynistic. Similarly, men who choose to only top because bottoming would be too "girly" or "gay" may be indicating that they are holding onto some internalized homophobia on some level. Now some men experience real and significant pain when bottoming and choose not to on that basis. Some men simply have no desire for penetrative sex at all. It can take time to explore all that is sexually available with another man, and it may take several attempts to learn enough about your own body to know what feels right and what does not.

Apps and Online Dating

In today's world, dating usually begins online. Many of my clients wish they could meet someone naturally and out in public, but they still primarily pursue online connections. A gay man can choose from a huge number of dating apps. Many of these apps are primarily hook-up apps, which is important to understand. Remember that the healthiest approach to engaging these apps is for entertainment only. If a sexual or romantic connection results, that is just icing on the cake. Too often, people get sucked into perusing the apps for hours at a time, only to put them down, feeling horrible about themselves, about other people, or about both.

Many people use apps for a variety of different reasons and in various states of substance impairment. Some lie about who they are, what they look like, or what they want. Some seek targets to take advantage of for financial gain. An out-late man who is new to apps may be inundated with responses from very attractive younger men. These guys flirt and flatter, say everything a person may want to hear, and may even meet up for a bout of wild sex. Not long into knowing each other, requests for help paying a cell phone bill or the like may begin, or even requests for large sums of money. A definite and necessary learning curve exists to use apps successfully.

The best-known app for gay men is Grindr, but there are many more like it: Scruff, Adam4adam, Jacked, Hornet, Growler, etc. Some websites also exist for purely sexual connections, such as Squirt.org and Sniffies.com. Because they are website-based and not app-based, they have fewer restrictions on content. People use the majority of these apps and sites to set up sexual encounters, but some people are holding out for an actual date. Other sites that host people with all types of sexual identities include Tinder and Hinge, as well as others. Users may be slightly more interested in dating on these sites, but the chance someone is looking for a quick hookup is still great. Again, if a person has worked to understand their own values, what they want, and what they are available for, then they can better manage the emotional impact of these sites, as well as maintain a feeling of control. Do long-term, loving, committed relationships result from these sites? Absolutely they do, but they are not the rule.

Offline Dating

How does a person try to find a potential partner in a more successful way? A few approaches may improve the odds of success, although there are no guarantees. The first step is to cast a net that is wide enough but not too wide. We all have certain tastes and qualities we find more attractive, which are not to be ignored. If our list becomes too specific, we limit our options and eliminate the element of surprising ourselves. If I say I am looking for an Asian man between the ages of twenty-five and twenty-seven who is exactly five-foot, seven inches, holds an advanced degree and a successful job, owns a home and car, maintains a flourishing relationship with his whole family, follows a committed faith practice, and loves feet, I set myself up for failure in the dating world. In fact, when someone has a list so impossible, it usually is an indicator that they are indeed not yet available for a real relationship. Expand the parameters and widen the net, even if it is somewhat out of your comfort zone. Remember that dating begins with simply getting to know people, not actual dating. The more people you take time to get to know, the more you will come to know about yourself. The other practice that can help move dating offline is to imagine where the person you want to date may be:

> ➤ What are his shared interests with you?
> ➤ Where might he spend a Saturday morning or afternoon?
> ➤ What events or social locations might he attend that you would also enjoy?

By taking an inventory of activities you want to share with a partner, you generate a list of places and experiences to begin making connections.

One analogy for dating that I like is comparing it to job searching. You do some research and submit a lot of resumes. Sometimes, those resumes just disappear into the ether with no response. Some may get a quick no without much consideration. Others may lead to a phone screen which may lead to an interview. If that interview goes well, perhaps a second or third interview occurs. At that point, the answer may still be no on either side. Then one day, the answer is yes on both sides, and a new chapter begins. Dating often works the same way. And just like the process of interviewing can prevent a person from being in a mismatched job, dating also weeds out the relationships that ultimately wouldn't work anyway. Always remember that it is better not to be in a relationship than to be in a bad one!

Understanding Compatibility

When two people meet and feel chemistry, the feeling may be exciting and intoxicating. Walking on cloud nine and experiencing puppy love take over. Having these feelings in alignment with sexual identity may feel like winning the lottery! Thoroughly enjoy and treasure the feelings, but also keep them in perspective. Relationships take time to evolve, and getting to really know another person is a process. Sometimes in the highs of a new love, small or big red flags may be ignored. Feeling so happy makes it hard to know if one questionable action is representative of someone's general character or just a random mistake. Ultimately, as relationships begin, grow, and face various situations, we learn about lasting compatibility.

Two people will never be exactly alike in every way. Being in a relationship with someone who is absolutely identical would actually be somewhat boring and predictable. Two people get to know the ways they are alike and different in tastes, values, and worldviews. Sometimes, the differences are vast and become adversarial. Compatibility then becomes an issue with sustaining a relationship. Other times, the differences become enhancing to a relationship as they expand opportunities involving all kinds of issues. Couples need to face life challenges, big and small, to determine how they work as a couple. Those challenges don't always show up quickly or all at once, so being able to evaluate a level of commitment needs space and time. People sometimes label a relationship that lasts one or two years as a waste of time, but that is how long it takes to truly know and understand compatibility. Hopefully, a person can walk away from such relationships with important lessons about themselves that better prepare them for the next time around.

Relationship Options—Monogamy or Not?

Another term that is used frequently in the gay community is "open relationship." For many men first coming out, open relationships may be either off-putting or exciting. The reality, however, is that the term open relationship does not have one simple meaning. Two men in a relationship establish rules around their sexual behaviors, and they can revisit and reset those rules at any time without ending the relationship. This arrangement is called consensual non-monogamy.

Perhaps a better word to introduce with this concept is "fidelity." Fidelity defines the sexual boundaries within a relationship. Monogamy is the most commonly identified form of fidelity and the form most often expected in straight relationships. The gay community as a whole responded to historical discrimination and lack of equal rights by giving themselves access to freedoms that straight people were simply not allowed. Gay people developed a comfort level with less restrictive sexual boundaries within relationships, which was and often still is taboo in straight relationships. Monogamy can be a great and very healthy choice for any couple regardless of sexual identity, but human behavior shows that monogamy is hard over time. Straight men and women stray just like those in the queer community. The choice to explore an open relationship is often a way to relieve the stress valve related to cheating as well as to add some spice and spontaneity to a long-term sexual relationship.

The healthiest way to establish an open relationship is to first build a solid foundation of trust and love in the primary relationship. Opening a relationship to solve or avoid relational problems will almost certainly end in failure. The other requirement for maintaining a healthy primary bond is open and frequent communication. Ideally, a couple has an in-depth conversation about what fidelity will mean in their open relationship. Maybe they choose to sexually play with others together only. Perhaps playing with others separately is okay with agreed-upon practices. Once a defined fidelity is put into practice, couples should periodically evaluate how these boundaries feel in practice and make any adjustments along the way.

Most of my clients feel turned off by the idea of open relationships and avoid those who are in them initially, which is understandable and probably the best approach when newly dating. Occasionally, over time, an appreciation for the freedoms available to male couples will grow. Not everyone chooses this path, but they hopefully understand such choices without judgment. Ultimately, they choose what is right for them individually.

HIV+ Stigma in Dating and Sex

Men who are HIV+ will be part of the vast dating pool. Men who are negative or don't know their HIV status may refuse to pursue a romantic or sexual relationship with someone who discloses their status as positive based on fear of HIV. Without education about the realities of HIV today, such unnecessary and hurtful stigma will remain. Opportunities to develop a truly deep and valuable connection will be limited, and HIV fear may keep people from being tested regularly for HIV out of fear of being shunned.

I go in-depth into what HIV is and how it is medically treated in the next chapter on sexual health. It is important to understand that if an HIV+ person is undetectable, meaning their level of HIV is not currently detected in blood tests, they cannot transmit HIV. Having sex with them carries no greater risk of contracting HIV than with any other negative person who may or may not know his status. Most people who are positive get regular medical monitoring and, therefore, are actually some of the safest sex partners overall. Inner fears about this issue should be challenged with education and communication.

Do HIV+ men always disclose their status in advance, and should they? First of all, each person is responsible for their own sexual health. They should never make assumptions or totally believe what anyone else says about their own behaviors and status. A person may take every step available to protect themselves in sexual situations, regardless of their partner, and failure to do so increases the risk of all STIs. In that sense, it does not matter if someone discloses initially or not. Many people who are HIV+ do disclose their status prior to sexual contact. They may not disclose in initial interactions or on profiles. Many were emotionally hurt in truly awful and discriminatory ways while dating. Some prefer to get to know someone more deeply as a whole person before disclosure. This choice should never be met with judgment of any kind. It is informed by lived experience that should be acknowledged and respected. Many HIV+ men have the experience to quickly assess if statements from others, such as, "It doesn't bother me at all," are actually true. Respectful and honest dialogue about any hesitations when dating someone who is HIV+ is essential, as well as being willing to ask questions and learn a thing or two.

Fear about HIV was often part of what kept some men in denial, and so, fear about dating and sex with an HIV+ person understandably carries over in this process of change. Addressing this fear is another measure of whether someone is truly available for dating. If a person is holding onto their fears based on old ideas and is not willing to educate themselves about current realities, they likely are not totally available for true and deep connection.

Chapter 16:
HOW LUCKY YOU ARE

This letter was written by a man who came out at the age of forty after being married for fifteen years and fathering two children. He feared that he was way too old to ever find love and happiness after coming out. How very wrong he was.

Dear Me,

You are about to tell your wife of fifteen years that you are gay. You have known her since grade school. You went to the junior prom together. You have two beautiful children with her, a six-year-old daughter and a sixteen-year-old son. When you tell her, you hug each other very tightly. You both start to cry uncontrollably as she says, "I love you too much to ask you to stay."

The weeks and months ahead are a heart-wrenching limbo as you, your wife, and your kids create a new normal. Be prepared because it will be an emotional earthquake like nothing you will ever experience. You will rail at the Universe for making you gay because it means that you will hurt three people whom you love so deeply. You move two hours away for a new job/life and visit your soon-to-be ex-wife and children each weekend. You miss them. It tears you apart to see how much sadness and upheaval you are causing.

While this is happening, you are experiencing, for the first time in your forty years, what it is like to be openly gay. At first, you worry that you are too old and that no man will be interested in you. You soon learn that this is far from the truth. Going to the clubs will be exhilarating. You will feel so much joy being surrounded by so many gay men—humans who are like you. As you drive to work and rollerblade in the park, you feel happy to be alive. You will start to realize how heavy a weight you have been carrying around your entire life, trying to hide that you are gay. With this weight gone, you will feel a lightness of being that is like a drug.

You will have a lot of one-night stands and extended relationships. You will discover that there are a lot of gay men out there with a great deal of emotional pain. And then you meet that man at two o'clock in the morning at a club and spend the night together. That night will extend to a month, a year, and beyond. You will say, "I love you," and be blown away with joy at hearing that person, a man, repeat it back to you. You will marry this man and remind yourself daily how lucky you are.

During all of these years, your ex-wife and children will remain a big part of your life. They will heal. You will still love them, and they will love you back. They will meld into the new life you and your husband have created. A "Bonus Family" will form. You will spend holidays together, go to graduations together, plan weddings together, and comfort each other at the loss of loved ones. You will not regret not having come out sooner because by having been married and becoming a father, your life has turned out to be exceptionally rich and blessed.

Chapter 17:
SEXUAL ACTIVITY

This chapter may seem rudimentary to some, but having a frank and complete discussion about actual sex acts is important for many reasons. Learning to be comfortable talking about sex, desires, fantasies, etc., is integral to a complete and satisfying sex life for anyone. Understanding terminology and practice of all the ways men have sex with each other is also essential to feeling more comfortable with one's own sexuality. Many people hiding or denying their sexual truth may hold misunderstandings and misconceptions about how sex really works. Some learned about sex between men by watching pornography, but porn is a fantasy presentation that often neglects all the ins and outs, so to speak, that are part of the experience. I remember the first time I kissed another man when I was in college. While I carried all kinds of sexual fantasies for years about other men, I was totally unprepared for one thing: facial hair. I had only ever kissed women, and the feeling of another man's stubble on my face as we kissed was something that had never even occurred to me until it happened. It's absolutely no surprise that I liked it.

Sex Roles and Experiences

As always, it is best to start with some definitions, and the first is the definition of the word "sex." In sexual activity between a cisgender man and woman, a demarcation exists between sex acts that may lead to pregnancy and those that do not. Oral sex, anal sex, and mutual masturbation might be considered heavy foreplay, but vaginal penetration is likely considered "real" sex. In the grand scheme of things, engaging in any sexually arousing and pleasing acts is part of a sexual cycle that may or may not lead to penetration or climax, which we will define as sex.

Sex between men, like sex between any consenting adults, includes a range of experiences. Although pregnancy is clearly not a concern between two cisgender men, the perceived difference between penetrative sex and other sex acts still exists, with the latter often considered foreplay or fooling around. Often, ejaculation completes the definition of having had sex with someone when both or all partners are male, regardless of the exact engagements. Some men feel sexual satisfaction regardless of whether ejaculation occurs and may define any sexual interaction as a complete sex act.

Men often enjoy the simple pleasures of kissing and body contact as part of foreplay, although some men feel less comfortable with that level of contact when they are first experimenting or holding onto internalized homophobia. Some gay men hold the act of kissing to be much more intimate than any other sex act, and they reserve that for deeper connections. Just like with any person, internal systems develop around what feels natural, satisfying, and safe when it comes to sex, and trying to assign any sexual act as uniform and expected for all gay men is folly.

Most men had a sex life of some kind before coming out. They are likely familiar with masturbation (solo and perhaps mutual), oral sex, and penetration, most often with women. Gay men who never had sex with a woman refer to themselves as "gold star gays." A separate class exists for "platinum gays," meaning a man who was born by c-section and never had sexual contact with a woman, therefore never having touched a vagina. These classifications humorously sound like some kind of airline status. These terms are just some of the language one encounters as they make forays into dating and socializing with other gay men.

Anal Play and Anal Sex

The sexual topic most often associated with gay men is anal sex and anal play. Do all gay men engage in anal sex? No, they do not. Do some straight couples engage in anal sex? Yes, they do. Anal sex is not exclusive to gay men, and many of the practices, preparations, etc., we will discuss are applicable to anyone with an anus, which is everyone. Anal play for men is also a pathway for direct prostate stimulation, which can be immensely pleasurable. The prostate is often referred to as the male G-Spot. Discovering these new and titillating sensations can be an exciting area of experimentation for any man.

Many people have misgivings about anal sex as being "dirty" or "perverted," which often informs the hesitancy some closeted men feel as they start to explore this avenue of sexual expression. The anus contains a large concentration of nerve endings, which can make anal contact intensely pleasurable or intensely painful without proper preparation. Like genitalia, the anus can serve multiple roles in bodily function and sexual function. The anus and rectum can be cleaned just like any other body part to dispel some of the risks of having those functions overlap. Enema bottles or various douching products can be used to clean the rectum, and they can be found in drug stores or online outlets. When using an enema bottle, be certain to first empty out the laxative solution and replace it with simple water. If that option is unavailable, taking a shower and washing with soap while inserting a finger to clean the interior of the rectum can be helpful. Even with the best preparation, sometimes fecal matter can be released during anal sex. This should not be a cause of embarrassment or judgment. It can be easily and quickly cleaned up without having to end sexual activity in whatever form feels comfortable in the moment. A friend humorously offered, "If you are going to play in the backyard, you are going to get dirty sometimes!"

Once a level of comfort is attained with regard to cleanliness, next steps include getting familiar with the sensations that come along with anal play. I encourage clients to experiment while masturbating in order to get more familiar with their own bodies. One integral item is lubrication of some kind. Many types of lube are available for purchase, whether in an adult store or even online through Amazon or the like. The two most common options are either water-based or silicone-based. Water-based lube is generally less expensive and works better with condoms or toys. On the upside, water-based lubes will not stain. On the downside, they become rather gummy pretty quickly, thus requiring multiple applications. Silicone lubricant can be damaging to most sex toys, lead to breakage of condoms, and stain sheets and fabric. On the upside, it lasts much longer in use and will not become gummy. Use of either is a matter of personal preference. Different strokes for different folks, pun intended.

When exploring solo or with a partner, it is best to begin with stimulation on the outside with fingers (making sure fingernails are nicely trimmed) and then start to gently insert a single finger in order to grow accustomed to the sensation. At first, it is helpful not to touch your erection while inserting. When an erection is touched or rubbed, the sphincter naturally tightens and can make entry a bit more difficult. When first penetrated, it is also common to feel a burning sensation at first. Simply remove the stimulator for a few seconds and try again. The burning sensation passes quickly and usually will not return when insertion begins again. That simple exploration may be enough for a first experience. Once a person is ready for more, different options are available. Inserting more than one finger at a time to varying depths is the easiest next step. Penetrative toys or dildos can also be used, and they are available in many sizes and shapes. Some companies offer training butt plugs of increasing size to develop comfort along the way. Butt plugs are conical in shape with a taper and cap on the end, allowing for them to remain in place to develop some comfort and stretching. Whatever one chooses, start small and work up to longer and wider options. Some toys also have vibrating functions or certain curves that are designed specifically for prostate stimulation. Using toys and dildos can be very sexually exciting for couples or alone.

When the time comes to try entry with a partner's erection, the first step is to consider the use of a condom. The safest option is to use condoms correctly every time with any partner who is new or unfamiliar. Choosing not to use a condom increases the risk of all STIs. Medical experts recommend only having unprotected sex with monogamous partners once both have tested negative for any STIs.

Do not be too concerned about how long penetration lasts or whether it leads to ejaculation. Listen to your body and stay engaged as long as it feels good. Over time and with multiple attempts, a person learns more about how anal sex fits into their own preferences. One psychological barrier to monitor is whether internalized homophobia pushes hesitancy by believing that being the receptive partner is submissive or emasculating. Classic qualities of masculinity include a certain amount of toughness, grit, and risk-taking: no pain, no gain. In that sense, bottoming can be viewed as very masculine. Anal sex for either partner is simply a sexual expression that can feel great physically and emotionally and provide a deeper level of intimacy and connection in a relationship.

Another fairly common sexual practice between men is analingus, more commonly referred to as "rimming." An older euphemism is "tossing the salad." Oral stimulation or penetration of the anus using the tongue can be a very pleasurable and erotic experience for both the giver and the receiver. As with any type of oral physical contact, good hygiene is important before engaging in rimming for maximum enjoyment. Once again, this is a matter of personal preference and not a requirement for anyone. Rimming can provide a level of relaxation, excitement, and even lubrication that can make eventual penetration more comfortable.

Poppers

Some people use additional products designed to make anal sex more comfortable. Topical creams are available that can provide some numbing effect to minimize pain with initial entry. These products generally have minor effectiveness that is usually short-lived. Poppers are the most common product used by gay men for anal sex. Poppers are a liquid that is most commonly sold in small brown bottles that can easily be held in hand, and they have many different brand names. Poppers contain chemicals from the alkyl nitrate family, most commonly amyl. For use in anal sex, the aroma from the liquid is inhaled right before penetration, either directly from the bottle or from a rag that has absorbed some of the liquid. A rush follows quickly that usually feels like a warmth in the face, followed by some intense feelings of horniness.

The chemical itself relaxes stiff muscle fibers and so relaxes the anus as well. Relaxation and arousal are the benefits most sought from poppers when bottoming. As with any such product, it is important to weigh the benefits and risks. Most importantly, poppers are not physically addictive, and they are rarely used outside of sex. They can be a fun experience when used in moderation, and they can make initiating anal sex more comfortable. Some potential downsides include possible headaches shortly after use, as well as an increased heart rate that can be dangerous to anyone with high blood pressure or other heart issues. It is also dangerous for someone who also has taken erectile dysfunction medication, such as Viagra, as it doubles some of the effects on heart rate. The liquid itself can burn skin on contact and be very dangerous if it comes in contact with an eyeball.

Understanding language and regulations surrounding poppers is important. The name itself refers to early packaging that required popping a small bag with the liquid to release the aroma. The liquid was first used in the mid-1800s to treat angina. Today poppers face different levels of regulation that can vary by state and by country. Many regulations prevent use of the name poppers, so when shopping for them, that name is often avoided. The core ingredients are also found in leather cleaners and what was VCR head cleaners, and poppers are sold under that banner and with that nomenclature, although I don't know too many people who go to adult bookstores or the like to buy VCR head cleaner. Sometimes poppers are identified by brand names, such as Rush or Jungle Juice. Different countries around the world have varying policies, with some outright banning their sale and use. For anyone who is new to the world of sex between men, it is simply important to know some of the facts related to poppers, as their use is very common.

Helpful Resources

Sex is a topic that many like to joke about but rarely want to really talk about. Some find the topic embarrassing, and others are afraid to share what they don't actually know. Like any taboo or foreign topic, education and then communication are the best answer. There are many books available that explore all possible facets of the ways men have sex with each other. Here are a few that I would recommend:

> ➤ *The New Joy of Sex* by Charles Silverstein and Felice Picano
> ➤ *The Ins and Outs of Gay Sex* by Stephen Goldstein
> ➤ *Ultimate Gay Sex* by Michael Thomas Ford

One can also discuss questions, feelings, and confusions with a doctor or counselor well-versed in working with gay men. Learning to talk about these issues with professionals is actually a great way to rehearse these important eventual conversations with sexual and romantic partners.

Chapter 18:
SEXUAL HEALTH

For any single adult, regardless of sexual identity, it is important that individuals pay attention to sexual health. For those who have been away from dating for a long time or who are engaging in same-sex interactions for the first time, being aware of the spectrum of sexual risks, treatments, and safety practices becomes imperative to making the most informed choices. If you are coming out for the first time, it can be very beneficial to seek out a doctor who works comfortably and openly with the LGBTQ+ population. In many major metropolitan areas, doctors' offices may advertise in local publications that cater to the LGBTQ+ community. In smaller markets, take time to interview potential doctors about their experience working with gay men and their fluency with current medication and treatment protocols. Finding medical professionals who are comfortable answering questions and facilitating conversations about sexual health can be a huge asset in the coming-out process. We will walk through various health and sexual health issues common to gay men, but always rely first and foremost on the medical information provided by your own medical doctor.

HIV, AIDS, and PrEP

The first health issue that usually comes up related to gay men and sexual health is HIV and for a good reason. Undiagnosed and untreated HIV infections could potentially progress to AIDS and become fatal. In 2019, 690,000 people died of AIDS-related illnesses globally. In the United States, there were 34,800 new cases of HIV diagnosed in 2019, with an estimated 1.2 million people age thirteen and over living with HIV. The good news is that HIV no longer has to be a cause of premature death. It is possible to treat HIV simply with one or two daily pills that keep levels undetected. Currently, the CDC equates an undetectable HIV level with being non-transmissible. For many years, an HIV diagnosis was seen as a death threat. Today, that is no longer the case when diagnosed, treated, and managed. A few years ago, HIV+ individuals started to be diagnosed with Alzheimer's Disease for the first time. While this may seem like an odd fact to celebrate, it is an indication that people with HIV are living to normal life expectancy, and that is a reason for celebration.

Learning some basic information about HIV is foundational to making informed decisions about sexual health. Human Immunodeficiency Virus (HIV) is the virus that can cause Acquired Immunodeficiency Syndrome (AIDS), which can be deadly. AIDS is a separate medical condition from HIV that can develop when HIV is left untreated. HIV can be transmitted between people through four bodily fluids: blood, semen, vaginal fluid, and breast milk. One of the reasons it spread quickly through the gay community is because semen can transfer the disease most easily through mucous membranes that are found in the rectum. Unprotected anal sex was and is still the riskiest sexual behavior when it comes to HIV. Transmission cannot happen from semen to skin contact unless there is an open wound on the skin or in the mouth, and transmission rates are low in such circumstances. Additionally, the virus carried in semen only lives for a brief time in the open air. Is it possible to contract HIV through oral sex and swallowing semen? The answer is yes, it is possible, but the chances are much lower. It is recommended not to brush teeth or floss right before performing oral sex as that can open up small pathways in the gums. Know that there is no such thing as absolute safe sex; condoms are recommended for anal or oral sex. In reality, using condoms for oral sex is often overlooked, and the use of condoms during anal sex is sometimes overlooked in the heat of the moment. Ultimately, a person can take steps to protect themselves from HIV or any other STI for that matter. No one can tell if another person has an STI from looking at them, so decisions must be made individually according to the level of risk a person wants to take.

A vaccine for HIV has been the holy grail for medical researchers for decades now. Progress has been very challenging and slow, but further advances are reported all the time. Fortunately, in the absence of a vaccine, a preventative treatment was developed with significant protective abilities, depending on how closely protocols are followed. This treatment is most widely known as PrEP (pre-exposure prophylaxis) and is known under the brands Truvada and Descovy. This medication is a form of the same medications to treat HIV, and reports compiled by the CDC describe prevention rates from ninety-six to ninety-nine percent during sexual contact. The treatment regimen involves taking a pill once a day, roughly at the same time daily, and requires blood tests for HIV through the prescribing doctor every three months. As with any medication, the risks of side effects should be considered. Because it is not 100 percent effective, doctors also recommend the continued use of condoms. Once again, in reality, many gay men take PrEP in order to not use condoms for sex. Do they still run a small risk of contracting HIV? Yes, they do. Every person gets to make their own decisions about what level of risk is most comfortable for them.

Fortunately, a person taking PrEP is tested regularly for HIV and other STIs, so they are actually more informed about their own sexual health. Who should take PrEP given that it has health risks like any other medication? Anyone who has regular unprotected sex with strangers should definitely be taking PrEP if they are medically able. Someone in a sexual relationship with someone who is HIV+ should also be taking PrEP. What about men in committed relationships or men who are very careful about with whom they have sex? This decision should always be made in consultation with a person's doctor, and there are no absolute rights or wrongs. One thing to consider, however, is that we can never be totally certain our partners tell the truth about their histories or their behaviors. And while having HIV is no longer a death sentence or even a huge inconvenience, not having it is still physically healthier overall. Unfortunately, stigma also still exists, even in the gay community, about being positive. This is tragic, discriminatory, and unfair, but it does exist, as noted in the earlier section on dating and HIV. If taking one pill a day provides the most protection when combined with other lifestyle choices, it can be hard to argue against it even when considering any possible side effects.

If exposure to HIV occurs unexpectedly, haphazardly, or neglectfully in a sexual encounter, emergency treatment is available, but it must be started within the first seventy-two hours after exposure. The sooner the treatment begins, the greater the level of protection against potential infection. The treatment is Post Exposure Prophylaxis (PEP). Medications are taken daily for twenty-eight days, and some nausea is a possible side effect. PEP should never be used as an alternative to condom or PrEP use.

Bacterial Infections—Syphilis, Gonorrhea, Chlamydia

Outside of HIV, there are many sexually transmitted infections that need to be kept in mind when maintaining sexual health. As a rule, the only way to prevent infection is to abstain from sexual contact completely. Short of that, correct use of condoms every time for every sex act is the most effective way to prevent the transmission of STIs. Dental dams or a condom that is cut open can be used for added protection for rimming as well. In real-world practice, not many people use protection for oral sex or rimming, and one simply must be willing to take the risk of exposure with those activities. We will look at some of the most common STIs from both a transmission and treatment perspective so that the most informed decisions can be made. We will also look at certain vaccinations that gay men should consider.

Gonorrhea, also known as the clap, is a highly transmissible STI that is common in both straight and gay communities. The good news is that gonorrhea is generally easily treated with medication, although some strains are becoming resistant to antibiotics. Gonorrhea is a bacterial infection usually spread through sexual fluids such as semen. An infection can happen in the penis, anus, mouth, or even the eyes. Symptoms may include a burning sensation when urinating, white, yellow, or green discharge from the penis or anus, or anal itching, soreness, or bleeding. Many men have no symptoms at all, which is why regular testing when sexually active is important as it will not clear up on its own. Gonorrhea can be detected through either a urine sample or a blood test. Treatment usually consists of a single shot of antibiotics.

Chlamydia is another bacterial infection that is spread through sexual fluids and can lodge in the penis or rectum with similar symptoms to gonorrhea. Antibiotic treatment also can clear the infection. If left untreated in men, the infection can lead to fever and some damage to the tubes attached to the testicles. Chlamydia is also detected through laboratory tests from urine samples or swabs.

Syphilis is a progressive bacterial infection that is spread through direct contact with a syphilis sore. These sores can develop around the penis, rectum, or mouth, and they may be hard to see if small and hidden behind hair or skin folds. Syphilis develops in stages and can lead to serious health conditions if untreated. Testing is through blood samples, urine, or swabbing of a visible sore. Once again, regular testing when sexually active is important as many men can go years without any notable symptoms. If the infection advances, it can lead to brain and nerve issues, eye problems, and even blindness. The good news is that syphilis is easily treated with effective antibiotics.

Other Viral Infections: Herpes, HPV, and Monkeypox

Three other viruses beyond HIV exist that transmit through sexual activity. The first is herpes, both genital and oral. According to the CDC, oral herpes is present in fifty to eighty percent of the U.S. population and leads to what are known commonly as cold sores. Genital herpes can result in similar sores in the genitals, anus, and rectum, and it is estimated that more than thirteen percent of the world's population is infected with genital herpes. The oral version can be transmitted to the genital areas when a mouth sore is present.

Because herpes is a virus, it has no permanent cure. Once infected, a person will continue to carry the virus, although it may be dormant for long periods of time. Medications are available that can shorten the time sores are present and may help prevent outbreaks and transmissions when taken regularly. Many people are horrified when they first receive a diagnosis, but it is important to remember that herpes, both oral and genital, are very common. Being able to communicate with sexual partners about this should be free from stigma. Like syphilis, the greatest risk is when sores are present, which opens up exposure to additional infections, including HIV.

Human papillomavirus, or HPV, is another sexually transmitted virus. HPV can lead to genital warts that may appear around the penis or the anus and rectum and also carries some risk of cancer in the penis or anus. Many people, however, carry HPV with no symptoms at all. The CDC does not even recommend testing for HPV in men without any symptoms present, so many doctors do not screen for it. HPV is very common in many adults regardless of sexual identity. A vaccine was developed that is now routinely offered to young people in efforts to reduce the transmission. Women have a higher risk of cervical cancer caused by HPV, so efforts are being made to reduce transmission in the young. Gay men or men who have sex with men under thirty-five should consider being tested and vaccinated if appropriate to provide the highest level of protection.

The final virus we will consider is monkeypox. Up until 2022, monkeypox was mostly contained on the continent of Africa. It was first detected in 1958, and transmission was almost exclusively from animal to human. A vaccine was developed and administered only in populations of Africa that were considered to be most at risk. Monkeypox outbreaks were recorded in the U.S. in 2003 and

2021, but in 2022, monkeypox began to spread primarily through human-to-human transmission for the first time. Original outbreaks tended to center on men who have sex with men. The virus is not classified as an STI at the time of this writing. The virus more traditionally begins with flu-like symptoms followed by an outbreak of a rash on the face or extremities. In the current global outbreak, the rash appears on the genitals and anus as well. Much like herpes, the monkeypox rash results in blisters that eventually pop and heal over. The duration of the viral effects lasts two to four weeks. The virus is known to spread through skin-to-skin contact with the rash and blisters, by the exchange of respiratory droplets with prolonged face-to-face contact, and through intimate physical contact, such as kissing or cuddling. Like any virus, there is no cure, but antiviral drugs developed to protect against smallpox may be used to treat monkeypox infections.

Vaccinations to Consider

Certain vaccinations that are not given as a matter of course in childhood should be considered by gay men. Because of risks related to anal sexual contact, gay men have a higher chance of being exposed to both hepatitis A and B, although both are relatively rare. A series of vaccines can be given to prevent both forms of hepatitis. They are usually given in multiple doses over six months, and immunity can only be reached once all doses have been administered. As previously mentioned, vaccination for HPV exists but is usually only administered to men below the age of twenty-six. Those age limits are under review, and sexually active gay men under thirty-five should consider asking for screening and vaccination from their health care provider. Finally, all gay men and men who have sex with men should seriously consider the vaccine for monkeypox, even if they received the smallpox vaccine in childhood. The smallpox vaccine was discontinued in 1972 when the disease was considered eradicated. The monkeypox vaccine is given in two doses, four weeks apart.

Chapter 19:
RISKS OF SUBSTANCE ABUSE

One of the pitfalls when coming out is the increased risk of substance abuse or dependence. If one has a personal or family history of alcoholism or addiction, it is imperative to keep an eye on these behaviors. The idea that all gay men are heavy drinkers and drug users is one of the insidious myths that simply is not true. Having said that, it is true that gay bars are the most common "watering holes" for gay people to meet and socialize freely and comfortably. While dating apps and the like impacted the role gay bars play in finding dates or sexual partners, they remain a hub for group socialization. When a person comes out later, going to gay bars is often part of the rituals to experience being out and open. When that same person walks in with nervousness and trepidation, turning to a few drinks to relax is quite normal.

Why Pay Attention to This?

Developing a circle of friends in a partying environment is also quite normal and often very helpful and rewarding when first coming out. In my practice, however, some clients quickly get caught up in a routine that includes heavy drinking on a regular basis. Their initial friendships and relationships in that setting can become volatile and not end well. Many clients talk about arguments and hurt feelings occurring again and again in these new relationships but only when inebriated. The partying can be a fun outlet for a while, but it is an area that can become so central to socializing that it starts to negatively impact other aspects of life.

Studies from the Substance Abuse and Mental Health Services Administration (SAMHSA) show that rates of substance abuse, including alcohol, tend to run higher in marginalized communities, including the gay community. This is not a character flaw but more a response to the stress faced by discrimination and the fear of being judged or harmed by the majority culture. All people struggle to handle stress and judgment, and leaning on substances or behaviors for relief is quite common regardless of personal identifiers. When those feelings are amplified, especially by the forces that kept someone in denial and in the closet, the risks also amplify, so paying attention to how and why one is using mood-altering substances while in the coming-out process is very important.

Types of Substances and Their Impacts

Related to drinking patterns, a person may find himself exposed to the use of drugs of various kinds for the first time. Cannabis, mushrooms, cocaine, G or GHB (gamma-hydroxybutyrate), K (Ketamine), ecstasy (Molly), and meth are not uncommonly used in some gay settings.

Again, this is not at all unique to gay socialization, but for someone who spent years avoiding a social life, this may be their first exposure. Some may have a curiosity about the sensations, and others may feel a certain pressure to try things to fit in with a crowd (another aspect of a second adolescence). Basic education about the risks related to various drugs is very important. Both cocaine and meth can become addictive almost immediately for some. A person's mind and body can immediately start to crave more and more of the substance, quickly requiring larger and larger amounts for the same effect. While hallucinogens such as mushrooms, K, and G may not have the same physical craving response, they can start to become required to feel comfortable socializing. Whether or not cannabis is addictive is a topic of disagreement in professional, medical, and behavioral health arenas, but when its use becomes mandatory to engage socially, it often mirrors the same level of addiction and destruction as any other drug.

I bring up this warning because I watched men with literally no history of alcohol or drug abuse move into a high level of addiction and destruction within months of first use. One client began exploring his sexuality with other men while married, and pursuing those connections themselves became addictive once he started to include using drugs. He had a family history of addiction, but he had never engaged in use before in his life. His behaviors led to a precipitous fall, the discovery of all of his behaviors by his wife, and a loss of his job. He started therapy at a very low point, and we began the work of self-acceptance. That work, however, was stymied by his ongoing, active substance addiction. He was in denial about his addiction, just as he had been about his sexual identity. His progress was inconsistent, and he remained unwilling to address his substance use directly. His divorce became protracted and extremely expensive and difficult, and he stopped engaging in any therapy at all. This story has no happy ending to report, at least not yet. This story is an example of why paying attention to substance use is vital when taking this emotional journey.

One drug, in particular, meth, needs to be understood in terms of how it is used by gay men and its destructive power on lives and relationships. Meth is a powerful party drug within some circles of gay men. It can be highly addictive from the first use, and it can spiral out of control in no time. Meth can be smoked, snorted, or injected. Regular meth use wreaks havoc on appearance, much more so when smoked. Meth can rot teeth and the jawbone and leave the face looking decades older. Many gay men prefer to inject meth with the belief that they will be able to preserve their good looks. They will not.

The use of meth by gay men is closely tied to sex, making its appeal all the greater. People who have developed an addiction, which they believe they have under control, usually live in use cycles. They plan for one to four days over a weekend of using and coming down. During the using time, they do not eat and must plan to hydrate and take vitamins to stay functional. Under the influence, they stay awake for days on end and engage in near-constant sexual activity with a multitude of men. The fall from the high is extreme and hard. The abuse of their body leads to rapid weight loss and impacts organ functioning and blood pressure. Their risk of STIs goes up exponentially, and the addition of other drug or alcohol abuse is very common. Their relationships tend to fail, and their jobs become at risk as their performance plummets. No happy endings exist in these stories without help to recover once addiction takes hold. Meth is not a drug that is recreational, no matter what anyone tells you. If you date someone, and they reveal that they use meth on occasion, run for the hills immediately. If they share that they used to use meth, sought treatment, and have a long record of sustained sobriety, then go for it.

I have never used meth, nor have I been in a relationship with anyone who has. But in my work, I have seen first-hand the devastating effects this drug has on people and those who love them. I had one client who attended several rounds of rehab related to his meth use, but he could not find a way to free himself from this drug. Despite having married a wonderful man and adopting a beautiful son, he never found lasting recovery. One night, he injected what he thought was meth but was actually fentanyl, and he died alone on his bathroom floor.

Abuse and addiction can sneak in quickly, and it is important to be prepared. Some people indicate in profiles on apps that they are seeking this experience. They use PNP (Party and Play), parTy, or Tina in the text of their profiles or communications (crystal meth is often called T or Tina). If you have never tried meth, avoiding the first use is the absolute best-case scenario.

Help Is Available

If you find yourself struggling with substance use of any kind, it is vital to know that help is available in many formats that address the specific needs of the LGBTQ+ community. Many counselors, social workers, and psychologists provide treatment to assess and address substance use disorders. Treatment centers are also available to establish a foundation for recovery from addictions. The Pride Institute in Minnesota is dedicated to treatment for the LGBTQ+ community exclusively, but many centers around the country include programming specific to the LGBTQ+ demographic. A little research may be required to see what help is available near you. Many people in the

LGBTQ+ world feel more comfortable seeking help when they know that their sexual identity will be accepted and understood. Twelve-step programs, such as Alcoholics Anonymous, Narcotics Anonymous, or Crystal Meth Anonymous, also exist for all substance use that can be very successful in providing and supporting recovery. Some cities have clubhouses that host twelve-step groups specifically for LGBTQ+ individuals. Once again, there are reasons why finding such meeting groups is valuable.

Twelve-step programs include knowing and relying on a "higher power," which is often referred to as "God." Due to the ways that religion may have harmed members of the LGBTQ+ community, many have a hard time with this aspect of this recovery approach. Meeting and learning from others who have walked this path reveals the many ways that a "higher power" can be understood in a non-religious context. A simple search online for recovery support in a specific area should provide a good collection of resources for help, and some options can be found in the appendix.

Section Four:
COMING TRUE

Chapter 20:
LIVING AUTHENTICALLY

Authenticity is a buzzword found in discussions about mental health and having a healthy self-esteem. What does authenticity really mean, and how does it relate to sexual identity? The psychological definition of "authenticity" refers to the attempt to live one's life according to the needs of one's inner being rather than the demands of society or one's early conditioning. In terms of sexual identity, this reflects living in a way that does not deny the totality of self across all sectors of life, regardless of what others may think or how they may judge. Living authentically does not mean a gay person must disclose their sexual identity in all situations. It does mean no longer taking a position of hiding or denial when this aspect of life becomes part of normal social discourse, such as sharing honestly about life events with a friend, family member, or even a trusted coworker.

When coming out later in life, we need to teach the people in our lives how to talk about it. If we never share anything from our personal lives, we subtly communicate that this aspect of who we are is somehow suspect or needs to be kept in the shadows. Some fear that talking about their personal or romantic life could make someone else uncomfortable, so it is best to avoid the topic altogether. Straight people never experience this. Choosing to live life authentically means no longer participating in that kind of shell game.

Privacy vs. Secrecy

All people have a right to privacy. Living authentically does not mean having to share every detail of one's personal life with everyone. All people use personal judgment about what to share and with whom based on their own values. The key is being honest about personal motivation. Secrecy and privacy are not the same things. Secrecy is laced with shame, fear, and embarrassment. Privacy is based on setting appropriate boundaries according to relationships. A parent probably will not disclose much about their dating life with their children but may do so more freely with friends. If a particular setting triggers internal alarms about potential conflict with people who are likely to become harshly judgmental or worse, holding cards close to the chest may be appropriate. In a workplace setting, if co-workers have personal photos of family and spouses on display, feel free to do the same. No hard and fast rules exist about the right amount of self-disclosure; it is just important to explore whether those choices are being made from a place of fear and shame or from a place of healthy boundary setting.

Inventory for Change

One way to start living authentically with regard to sexual identity is to make what I call an inventory for change. This step is best engaged once

a person is far enough down the line in coming out to have some perspective on the experience rather than in the midst of so much change.
The inventory involves taking a thorough, honest look at ways hiding
from honesty and acceptance about sexual identity hurts or causes
damage to both self and others. This examination is an opportunity
to take personal ownership and accountability for all that happened.
In doing so, one can more clearly chart how they want to show up
in life from this point forward. The first part of this book explores
all of the various forces that lead people to seek refuge in denial and
secrecy. Understanding, acknowledging, and accepting the role those
forces played is critical to growth. Truly healing and creating this new
life direction, however, requires not using those forces as excuses or
justifications for the ways we and others were hurt along the way. We
must recognize the deeper aspects of ourselves that ultimately gave in to
those external forces. Once we identify those deeper places, we can then
create a roadmap for change that guides our journey to authenticity.

Perhaps the most common and easily identifiable emotion that
led to this journey is fear. We were unable to face our fears for many
reasons, and so we made what seemed to be the easier and safer choices
for ourselves and others. At the time, these choices may have felt selfless,
putting the needs of others ahead of our own, but in reality, they were
actually selfish choices to avoid embarrassment and shame. Our ego
could not seem to handle the perceived hit from being seen and known
as gay. Our efforts to avoid our own internal shame and fear mani-
fested in trying to meet other people's expectations about who we were
"supposed" to be. We lacked the courage at the time to state or even
see our truth, and we moved ahead from that place of fear and shame.

As marriages happened and children may have been added to
the family, fear only amplified, along with an intricate system of

thoughts and behaviors to preserve deception of self and others. Countless opportunities probably came up along the way to look behind the curtain at the truth, but we had yet to find the courage to do so. Perhaps sexual explorations into our identity happened, and vows were knowingly broken and justified with faulty beliefs. These failures to self and others truly sit at their core in ego protection, self-centeredness, selfishness, and inconsiderate choices. Perhaps we were confronted directly about suspicions, and we denied them completely with a hint of judgment for even thinking such a thing could be true. Perhaps, when in the company of straight people, we joined in with the laughing at or demeaning of gay people that sometimes happens. Perhaps we joined in moral condemnation in religious settings, even when our personal behavior was contradictory to that which we publicly espoused. Regardless of the injustices we may have experienced from family, culture, and faith that buttressed denial, we ultimately made our own choices, and we must own those choices fully in order to heal and move forward.

Looking inward and accepting that we have been fearful, cowardly, and selfish in some aspects of our lives is incredibly hard. Moments of failure are not the whole story, of course. In many ways, on many days, we showed up with courage and selflessness as well. We did many, many good things that greatly benefitted those we love. Our denial and struggle to break free are not a story of complete failure of character. On the whole, we were decent people with good intentions and good hearts.

Mission Statement for Authenticity

We begin to chart a path that embodies authenticity by accepting the moments when aspects of ourselves failed to face fear or accept truth. This path may include the following steps:

➤ We commit to naming and facing our fears and then doing something about them rather than letting them fester.

➤ We are considerate about the ways our actions and decisions will affect the people we love, and we act to protect them and ourselves from harm.

➤ We step out of self-centeredness when it wants to show up, and we build our barrier-free connections through honesty.

➤ We use our internal barometer of what is right and true, and we name injustice when we see it.

Armed with acceptance and understanding of our flawed thinking and behaviors, we can now create a self-defined mission statement about who we want to be from now on. We are all just human beings, so we will fail at times on these commitments. We will be vigilant and honest about when that happens and quickly try to course-correct. Such a mission statement may declare:

I commit to being as honest with myself and others as I can be, to being true and consistent about who I am no matter where I am, to being a protector of myself and others like me, and to being willing to look at my own mistakes so that I may continue to grow closer to my best self.

A mission statement must be unique to a person's individual story and journey and must be measurable and achievable. The clearer and more honest the mission statement, the closer one will be to living an authentic life.

Chapter 21:
LETTING GO OF INTERNALIZED HOMOPHOBIA

Internalized homophobia (IH) has played a damaging part in the lives of men who come out later. IH impairs the ability to live wholly and authentically, attacks self-esteem, and bolsters the feeling of having nowhere to belong. Resolving this force is not completed by the act of coming out alone. Resolution requires a deeper investigation of the pockets where IH wants to hold on and continue its damage. Recognizing its role and power is essential to truly creating a life that is full and free. Every gay person does not have to share similar beliefs, attractions, and relationship styles in the long run. Letting go of IH means moving into accepting differences with respect rather than judgment. As we explore early in this book, the LGBTQ+ community is vast and varied, with a multitude of identities and lived experiences. What binds them together is living outside of heterosexual paradigms and seeking an equal place in society. If a gay man wants acceptance and respect for who he is, he lets go of judgments about other people seeking the same regarding their own identities. Holding onto those judgments displays hypocrisy that hurts all involved. Judgments about others' experiences are often rooted in the deepest pockets of IH and will only amplify feelings of being "other than" rather than "part of."

Differences and Deficits

We start working on IH by recognizing that differences within a group are wider than the differences between groups. If we take straight men as a group and gay men as a group, it is somewhat easy to identify the real difference between these groups: who and what they find sexually and affectionately attractive. Describing straight men as "masculine and manly" and gay men as "feminine or girly" is entirely untrue and also implies that femininity is somehow a weakness. If we look at all straight men as a group, some may be described as "masculine" while others may be described as more "feminine" in demeanor and interests. Some are very religious, and some are atheists. Some are politically conservative, and others are politically liberal. Some value ambition and financial success, and some value purpose without care of financial reward. All of these differences, and the many more that exist, can be applied to gay men as a group as well. The differences within the group are vast.

The next important factor to consider is that we are all trained and socialized to believe that difference must equal deficit. When we have two different items, we must somehow force rank them, with one being better than the other. As children, we are graded and ranked by school performance. In sports and academic competitions, we are ranked and placed as winners or losers, best or worst. We may be taught that our own religious beliefs are right and correct while others are false and immoral. Historically and systematically, we may have been taught that male was better than female, white was better than non-white, and certainly, straight was better than non-straight. Stepping into force ranking differences is often automatic and internal for many people.

Marginalized groups fight hard to challenge these implied deficits. Civil rights struggles, whether addressing race, gender, or sexuality, battle to say that difference is not deficit but simply difference. Some struggle with balancing difference against their ideas of right and wrong, and at times, they overlap in thorny and challenging ways. When we explored faith issues about sexual identity, we brought to the surface the reality that religious teachings about right and wrong are often diametrically opposed to the desire to be whole and true as a gay person. IH wants a person to hold onto the belief that being gay is not just a difference, but it is less than in any possible comparison. IH has a unique hold when intersectionality is examined as well. I worked with clients of color who felt absolutely no shame or self-loathing regarding their race but very much so about their sexual identity. They recognized that discrimination is the problem when it comes to racial differences, but they still believed that being gay is the problem when it comes to sexual identity. If they could wave a magic wand and become straight, they would. If they could wave a magic wand and become white, they would not. It had not yet occurred to some that waving a magic wand that made being gay acceptable and respected in all situations is the solution they most want. IH wants a person to believe that their sexuality is the problem that needs fixing (or fixing up at the very least) not the distorted and bigoted attitudes of those who want to demonize this simple difference.

The last aspect of IH to consider is that all people have their own sets of values, beliefs, and opinions. Everyone has certain types they find more attractive, both relationally and sexually. These individual settings are never bad. For a gay man, he may find a masculine man attractive, or he may find a more feminine man attractive. He likely finds a multitude of personal qualities attractive that have nothing to do with masculinity or femininity. Having preferences when it comes to personal desires is healthy for all people. IH wants to assign judgments to anyone else's attractions that are different from our own.

Some elements of IH are more global and complicated. Disagreements in philosophy and beliefs will always exist between human beings, and struggles for equality between groups will continue. Equality is not finite, however, and gains for one segment of the population do not come at a cost to another segment. Demonizing differences—as if they are deficits—across groups is now normal in popular culture and society, so attempts to change this drive internally are even more challenging.

Messages from the LGBTQ+ community also have complicated implications about difference. Being gay and holding religious beliefs and practices can be viewed with suspicion, often the result of harm people have received in religious settings. Being gay and holding conservative beliefs about the size and role of government can be treated with outright derision, again often as a reaction to efforts to limit rights and security for LGBTQ+ people. These messages also affect IH in that one can resent their own sexuality because their personal beliefs may lead to exclusion in communities of other gay people, resulting in the feeling that there is no place to belong.

Steps to Recognize and Fight IH

So how does a person recognize when IH shows up after coming out? The answer is varied. Do you feel judgment about other gay people who present differently in demeanor or belief? Gay men will sometimes refer to someone as "very" gay, usually implying that the person in question meets the most derided stereotypical qualities associated with being gay. Being gay is not a matter of degrees; either you are gay, or you are not. Deriding or judging another gay man because of appearance, demeanor, gender expression, relationship style, or sexual role is usually an indication that IH is active. Noting or having feelings about these differences is not bad. Placing negative judgment on others out of fear that you will be ascribed those same qualities, however, is at the heart of IH. Using the language of absolutes about LGBTQ+ people, such as "all" or "always," is also an indicator that IH is alive and well. IH, at its core, is based on the fear that others will make absolute judgments about a person based solely on their sexual identity. That fear is often unfounded, but it is also not without some validity. Judgments come from people outside the LGBTQ+ community as well as from those within it. The secret is to recognize that those judgments are the problem, not sexual identity.

By striving to release the power of IH internally, a person must first practice the acceptance and equality that they want for themselves. Differences should be respected and not demonized. No one needs to cede personal beliefs about right and wrong. No one has to alter the "who, what, when, where, and why" of building relationships in all aspects of life. Letting go of IH does mean never accepting shame for this one aspect of identity and never communicating shame to others for the individual aspects of their own identity. Living without IH may mean taking the high road when faced with derision, but it does not mean failing to stand up for yourself and for right when needed. In taking steps to identify and challenge the myriad ways that IH may show up, a person will enhance self-esteem and help heal the hurt from IH and external homophobia.

Chapter 22:
THE REAL MEANING OF PRIDE

The term "Pride" in the LGBTQ+ community is accompanied by all kinds of imagery and a call to activism. June is "Pride Month" in the United States, and many cities have large parades and weekend-long celebrations. Smaller communities around the country hold different Pride events as well. In the city of Atlanta, where I live, Pride takes place in October in connection with National Coming Out Day. A few hundred thousand people gather for a weekend of parties, educational events, and community outreach. A giant parade winds through midtown filled with floats from churches and businesses, elected officials and political candidates, live television coverage, protesters and those who counter them, and a generally lively and festive atmosphere. Huge corporate sponsors line up, and big-name artists perform in concert. Every letter in the alphabet soup is represented with excitement and flair. Some cringe at what seems to be businesses capitalizing on Pride for financial gain, and others welcome the notoriety. These types of events happen in many places all over the world.

At the same time, people gather and march for Pride in some very unwelcoming corners as well. Many countries still outlaw homosexuality in action and word, punishable with imprisonment or death. Incredibly brave people literally risk their lives to stand up and be seen in hopes of moving the needle of acceptance in lands of intolerance. While some of the huge and elaborate celebrations elsewhere may no longer be rooted in such struggles, they do serve as a beacon of hope for those still waiting for a taste of freedom and safety.

Pride as an Event

The idea of a Pride parade was born from the Stonewall Riots in New York City. Groups of LGBTQ+ identified people banded together, led mostly by the transgender community, to literally fight back against the oppressive and violent tactics of law enforcement. They amplified the visible and audible movement for LGBTQ+ rights brewing in America. Those first parades and marches were not simply fun and colorful displays of freedom. They were passionate and committed actions to stand and be seen and to demand rights afforded to straight people. Pride became a call to action that lives and thrives today. Much progress has been accomplished by the earliest leaders and all who followed, but much more work is needed around the world before LGBTQ+ people can live, work, and love freely and safely in any corner of society.

Pride and Identity

Take a step back from the history of Pride as an event and action, and consider what Pride represents on the individual level as well.

The word "pride" has positive and negative connotations. There is the idea of feeling proud of oneself or someone else, and there is the idea of being proud as arrogant and boastful. Pride can be compassionate and admiring, or it can be vain and spiteful. So, what role does "pride" play in sexual identity development and overall identity? I believe that pride in this arena actually means living free from shame. It is less about being proud of being gay, per se, and more about rejecting any feelings of shame for being gay. It is about knowing and believing that one's sexual identity is as encoded and natural as the color of one's eyes.

I have blue eyes. I did not choose my eye color; I was born with it. Some people like blue eyes, others prefer brown eyes, others prefer green, and some could care less. I am not proud of having blue eyes, but I also feel no shame for it. The color of my eyes does not prevent me from getting a job, from being welcome in a community of faith, from loving who I love, from having or adopting a child. Family, culture, and faith do not ridicule or condemn me for my blue eyes. Blue is the color of my eyes, not the definition of how I see myself or how others see me.

If I live without shame about my sexual identity, then that same paragraph translates this way:

I am gay. I did not choose to be gay; I was born with it. Some people prefer gay people, some prefer straight, some prefer bi, and some could care less. I am not "proud" of being gay, but I also feel no shame for it. Being gay should not prevent me from getting a job, from being welcome in a community of faith, from loving who I love, from having or adopting a child. Family, culture, and faith should not ridicule or condemn me for being gay. Gay is my sexual identity, not the definition of how I see myself, and it should not be how others see me.

Notice the only difference between these two paragraphs is one says "does not," and one says "should not," which is where the concept of real pride comes into play in the lives of LGBTQ+ people. Until the day where that paragraph can be written identically, there is work to be done, things to teach and learn, and roles big and small to play in getting ourselves and our world to a place where we are no longer called to pride or shame for this aspect of who we are. We simply are who we are in the myriad facets that make us all human beings.

Chapter 23:
YOU DID IT

This last "Dear Me" letter is one I wrote to myself. I shared some points in my life that coincided with elements in this book, and now I want to share some of the rest of the story. As I described in the section on sexual abuse, after receiving help and treatment for PTSD, I began to realize and accept that, at my core, I felt sexual and affectional attraction for other men. I held onto the idea of being bisexual, and my faulty belief about being able to handle it kicked in. I also carried the deep fear that revealing this would only end in utter destruction for myself and those I loved. Now I see that I predictably moved into a deeper depression, greater isolation, and a general state of agitation as I tried to maintain the illusion.

At this same time, through a series of events, we became aware that our daughter was also coming into acceptance of herself as not being straight. The courage and strength she displayed as a young teenager moved me deeply, and the weight of carrying my own secret became more and more unbearable. My sense of despair was not lost on my wife, and she supported me in getting help. I worked with a counselor who helped me start to better understand my reality and the options that may be available. Oddly, it was my wife who first broached the subject. We were having dinner alone while on a family vacation, and she asked me point blank if my sexuality was an issue. She had done some research on my therapist and saw that he worked with gay and bisexual men. Once again, her bravery became the bar that I had to try to reach, so I told her that yes, my sexuality was the issue I was wrestling with. This began several very difficult weeks where she waited patiently for me to say my essential truth: I am gay. I sat on the edge of our bed in tears, and she held me tightly. As I described earlier, she is an angel from heaven. We made the heart-wrenching decision to end our marriage to give us both the freedom to live fully as who we are.

The following years are sometimes a blur. There was so much change in such a short time. I began drinking heavily, and my behaviors became erratic and unkind at times. I was relieved to be out and honest, but I struggled to find my footing. During this time, I also found deep love with another man with a similar history to my own. With time, patience, and forgiveness, we reached the place we are today, and it was worth it.

We share an amazing life together that is rich, exciting, fun, and deeply intimate. We have four children between us, and they are all fantastic people who have accepted our relationship fully. I now live a sober life, which enhances my ability to love and accept myself. Our former wives displayed unbelievable grace to us, and we remain real friends. Reaching this place did not happen overnight; it required a great deal of effort and sacrifice all around. Today, I am grateful to live an incredibly blessed life. The following captures the most important things I would have liked my younger self to know.

Dear William,

I know you are scared. Let's be honest: you are terrified! This feels like THE fork in the road of all possible forks in the road. Right now, all you can see is loss ahead, but you also know that continuing to live with this fear, shame, and pain is slowly killing you inside, day by day. It may feel like you will just be switching one pain for a new pain, but there is so much more in store. You have no idea how much you and your world will grow in the years ahead. You are not wrong that stormy and scary days and nights will be involved. Growing pains are very real. But I assure you, although right now you will not believe it, that you are stronger than you know and loved more deeply than you have ever been able to let in. You will survive. In fact, you will thrive.

I first want you to hear clearly that you are not broken, damaged, or flawed beyond repair. You are about to have the opportunity to become all of who you are, just as you were always meant to be. No more hiding, evading, censoring, or lying. No more trying to be what you believe everyone wants and expects you to be instead of who you really are. No more waiting in fear for the day it all comes crumbling down.

You know you married and have loved a strong woman with an incredible intellect and an even bigger heart. You invested in loving and raising your children, and they are stellar human beings. You worked hard to be a good person to family and friends. Sharing your truth will change things for sure, but it will not change any of those facts. One of the most surprising things that will happen is that all of those people will now have space to be even closer to you because you tore down the barrier you built around your whole self.

This transition will be rocky. Moments will come when you have no idea what to do next, when you have no clear answers for yourself or others, where you feel intense loneliness, and where you question if all this was worth it. Your wife will console you and revile you. She will cry and question everything, and her pain will feel like acid on your skin. And she will love you, too, as best she can in spite of all that is happening in her world. The days leading to your divorce will feel like having your skin ripped off, and the days after will feel like a relief. This will not be for the faint of heart, but remember again, you are stronger than you know.

AND—welcome to the rest of your life! You will have a true demarcation point between before coming out and after coming out. In some ways, it will feel like two different lives, but ultimately, it is just one very interesting, wild, and beautiful journey. You will fill out life with new people who only know you on this side. You will find professional direction that is in alignment with who you are. You will know romantic love to the depths of your soul, and you will have an expanded family with more people to love and love you back. All the "crap" of life will happen just like it always has, and your relationships all around will evolve and change, just like they would have anyway. But one day, my friend, you will look in the mirror and love who you see. You will say, "I did it." You will know you are stronger than you ever imagined, and you will know true peace. You will breathe deeply, love completely, and be whole.

APPENDIX

How to Find a Therapist

Regardless of the impetus to understand and deal with acknowledging being gay, the most important task is to work toward acceptance of self and the journey it took to reach this turning point. Sharing and processing this change with others is very hard without reaching peace and understanding on the inside first. Even when outed unexpectedly, taking time to self-examine is vital in moving through these choppy waters. Seeking professional help from a psychologist, counselor, or the like, who has experience and training working with gay clients, is tremendously helpful. Finding the right and appropriate fit is important, so let's look at how to assess the choices available.

If you look up "therapist LGBTQ+ and *insert your hometown*" online, some names will appear. COVID forced providers to offer virtual therapy, and many continue to provide that as an option. Looking beyond your hometown or even your state can be effective if there are few resources where you live. It is best to stick within your own state, at least, as they may have a deeper knowledge of local resources that may be helpful. Some providers may call themselves "coaches" instead. Coaching has no formal licensing, so you should be very thorough in researching the qualifications and experience of any coach to make sure they are the real deal.

Another resource to search for a therapist is *Psychology Today*, which can filter for insurance, location, and specialties. Some urban areas may have directories available for their specific area that only include therapists who attest to competency and training in working with the LGBTQ+ demographic. Local LGBTQ+ organizations or medical providers are also great options to query for recommendations. Sometimes, people will ask trusted friends or family for recommendations, or even through an employee assistance program (EAP) at work.

Once you develop a list of names that might work, call each and have an initial phone consultation to assess their experience and style. Feel free to ask about what percentage of their caseload identifies with the LGBTQ+ demographic, how many trainings or certifications they have received specific to issues in the LGBTQ+ community, and if they personally bring any biases for or against religion and sexuality. Be as specific in your questioning as needed for your particular circumstances. Engaging in therapy is an investment of time, emotion, and financial resources, and taking the time to kick the tires first is important. In these initial conversations, you will get a sense of personality and temperament as well, so pay attention to your gut in deciding who feels like a good fit.

A word of caution about professionals who may list LGBTQ+ as a population they see. Some professionals will check off that box when creating search profiles because they have no bias against the LGBTQ+ community and want to make that clear. It does not always mean that they have had specific training and experience with people coming out and how that process unfolds, hence the need for an interview where you can feel free to ask about their specific background and competency.

Resources for Coming Out Late

Online Resources and Organizations:

HRC.org

> "The Human Rights Campaign envisions a world where every member of he LGBTQ+ family has the freedom to live their truth without fear, and with equality under the law. We empower our 3 million members and supporters to mobilize against attacks on the most marginalized people in our community."

Pflag.org

> "PFLAG is the first and largest organization for lesbian, gay, bisexual, transgender, and queer (LGBTQ+) people, their parents and families, and allies. With nearly 400 chapters and 250,000 members and supporters crossing multiple genera-tions of families in major urban centers, small cities, and rural areas across America, PFLAG is committed to creating a world where diversity is celebrated and all people are respected, valued, and affirmed."

Books:

> ➤ *The Velvet Rage: Growing up Gay in a Straight Man's World* by Alan Downs
> ➤ *Fashionably Late: Gay, Bi and Trans Men Who Came Out Later in Life* by Vinnie Kinsella, editor

➤ *Finally Out: Letting Go of Living Straight* by Loren Olsen

Films:

➤ *Out Late*

➤ *For the Bible Tells Me So*

Resources for Religious Struggles

Faith Resources for Jews

Online Resources and Organizations:

Eshelonline.org

> "Eshel's Mission is to create a future for Orthodox lesbian, gay, bisexual, and transgender individuals, and their families. Through its innovative and culturally sensitive programming, Eshel works with each individual, family, and community in creating a place for their LGBTQ members. Eshel envisions a world where Orthodox LGBTQ individuals can live out their lives in the Orthodox community of their choice."

Keshetonline.org

> "Keshet envisions a world in which all LGBTQ Jews and our families can live with full equality, justice, and dignity. By strengthening Jewish communities by equipping Jewish organizations with the skills and knowledge they need to make all LGBTQ Jews feel welcome, we work to ensure the full equality of all LGBTQ Jews and our families in Jewish life. We also create spaces in which all queer Jewish youth feel seen and valued and advance LGBTQ rights nationwide."

Books:

➤ *Wrestling with God and Men: Homosexuality in the Jewish Tradition* by Steven Greenberg
➤ *Judaism and Homosexuality: An Authentic Orthodox View* by Chaim Rapoport

Films:

➤ *Trembling before G-d*
➤ *Keep Not Silent*
➤ *Hineini: Coming Out in a Jewish High School*

Faith Resources for Muslims

Online Resources and Organizations:

Algamea.org

"A human services organization established for support, socialization, education, and awareness in the Gay, Lesbian, Bisexual, and Transgender Middle Eastern Community."

Muslimalliance.org

"An organization working to support, empower, and connect LGBTQ Muslims."

Imaan.org.uk

"An organization based in the United Kingdom that supports LGBT Muslim People, their families and friends, to address issues of sexual orientation within Islam."

Books:

➤ *Queer Jihad: LGBT Muslims on Coming Out, Activism, and the Faith* by Jama Afdhere
➤ *Living Out Islam: Voices of Gay, Lesbian, and Transgender Muslims* by Scott Siraj al-Haqq Kugle

Films:

➤ *A Sinner in Mecca*
➤ *Naz & Maalik*
➤ *Circumstance*

Faith Resources for Christians

Online Resources and Organizations:

Qchristian.org

"We recognize that the church has not and does not always make it easy for those who identify as lesbian, gay, transgender, bisexual, same-gender loving, queer, pansexual intersex, asexual, genderfluid, or questioning to reconcile these aspects of themselves with their Christian identity. We are witnesses to both the harm that faith communities can inflict, and the hope and healing that is possible through Christ.

"By gathering together, embracing our differences, and celebrating our shared trust in God's love in Christ, we seek to point toward the full inclusivity to which God is calling us. Just as Jesus led by example in his life on earth, we are dedicated to living out a transformative example of fellowship in the world.

"Wherever you are on your journey, whether you are examining your own identity or walking along side others, you have found a place of welcome. We are grateful that God has brought you here, and we look forward to sharing the path forward together."

Reformationproject.org

"As a Biblke-bases, Christian organization, The Reformation Project's mission is to advance LGBTQ inclusion in the church."

Books:
- ➤ *God Believes in Love* by Gene Robinson
- ➤ *What's Morally Wrong with Homosexuality* by John Corvino
- ➤ *Clobber the Passages: Seven Deadly Verses* by Mel White
- ➤ *God and the Gay Christian* by Matthew Vines

Films:

- ➤ *For the Bible Tells Me So*
- ➤ *For They Know Not What They Do*

Resources for Substance Use Struggles

Pride-Institute.com

"Pride Institute offers inclusive and accepting recovery programs for members of the LGBTQ+ community. Pride first opened in 1986 and has since gone on to be one of the leading providers in the area of residential and outpatient program treatment for substance use and addiction needs of the LGBTQ+ population."

Twelve-Step Recovery Groups:

➤ Alcoholics Anonymous—aa.org
➤ Narcotics Anonymous—na.org
➤ Crystal Meth Anonymous—crystalmeth.org
➤ Alternative Recovery Resources:
➤ Smart Recovery—smartrecovery.org
➤ SAMHSA (Substance Abuse and Mental Health Services Administration)—samhsa.gov

Books:

➤ *Lust, Men and Meth: A Gay Man's Guide to Recovery* by David Fawcett, Ph.D.
➤ *Drugs, Sex, and Recovery: Fitting the Pieces Together* by Weston M. Edwards, PhD.
➤ *Alcoholics Anonymous Big Book* by Anonymous
➤ *Reclaiming Your Life: The Gay Man's Guide to Recovery from Abuse, Addictions, and Self-Defeating Behavior* by Rik Isensee

Resources for Gender Understanding

Online Resources and Organizations:

Translifeline.org

"Trans Lifeline provides trans peer support for our community that's been divested from police since day one. We are run by and for trans people."

Transequality.org

"The National Center for Transgender Equality advocates to change policies and society to increase understanding and acceptance of transgender people. In the nation's capital and throughout the country, NCTE works to replace disrespect, discrimination, and violence with empathy, opportunity, and justice."

Pflag.org

"PFLAG is the first and largest organization for lesbian, gay, bisexual, transgender, and queer (LGBTQ+) people, their parents and families, and allies. With nearly 400 chapters and 250,000 members and supporters crossing multiple generations of families in major urban centers, small cities, and rural areas across America, PFLAG is committed to creating a world where diversity is celebrated and all people are respected, valued, and affirmed."

Books:

➤ *Trans Bodies, Trans Selves: A resource for the Transgender Community* by Laura Erickson-Schroth, Editor

➤ *You and Your Gender Identity, A Guide to Discovery* by Dara Hoffman-Fox, Zander Keig, et al.

➤ *The Queer and Transgender Resilience Workbook* by Anneliese Singh

➤ *Gender Queer: A Memoir* by Maia Kobabe

Resources for Straight Spouses

Online Resources and Organizations:

Ourpath.org

"OurPath provides Straight Partners and Partners of Trans People with resources to cope constructively with the life-changing experience of disclosure or discovery. We provide a safe space for them to explore their own path toward a new normal. We help them navigate the challenges of rebuilding their identity, integrity and value system post-discovery or disclosure. We do this by providing individual and peer group support, a podcast, blog, and other online resources. We also reach out to the public and build bridges with organizations that promote LGBT+ equality to raise awareness about the Straight Partner experience."

Pflag.org

"PFLAG is the first and largest organization for lesbian, gay, bisexual, transgender, and queer (LGBTQ+) people, their parents and families, and allies. With nearly 400 chapters and 250,000 members and supporters crossing multiple generations of families in major urban centers, small cities, and rural areas across America, PFLAG is committed to creating a world where diversity is celebrated and all people are respected, valued, and affirmed."

Books:

➤ *The Other Side of the Closet: The Coming-Out Crisis for Straight Spouses and Families* by Amity Pierce Buxton, Ph.D.

➤ *Unseen-Unheard: Straight Spouses from Trauma to Transformation* by Amity Pierce Buxton, Ph.D.

➤ *My Ex is Having Sex with Rex* by Jennifer Lee

➤ *Annie's Story: How to Move Beyond the Pain of a Spouse's Homosexuality* by Annie Tulk

Acknowledgments

Several years ago, I began compiling certain themes and trends I noticed in the stories and experiences of the men I worked with in my Out Late group therapy. As I developed ideas, it became apparent that this information could help others in this situation more broadly. I began writing outlines that eventually became the table of contents for this book. I worked through several iterations, which led to this finished product. Many people helped me along the way.

Early in my professional career, some colleagues and I started meeting to see if there was a way to connect mental health professionals working with the LGBTQ+ community in Georgia. Melanie Storrusten, LCSW, Debonee Morgan, LMFT, Dee Desnoyers, Ph.D., LPC, and Pete Bell, LCSW, and I met repeatedly, leading to the creation of the LGBTQ Therapist Resource. Our work inspired me to see how counseling could reach beyond the walls of an office, and without it, I may never have been brave enough to write this book.

I also want to thank John Wilson, PsyD, for his help in my personal journey of coming out. Will Mahan, LPC, and Joe Remillard, Professor of Art at Kennesaw State University, generously gave of their time to critique my writing. My daughter, Maggie, provided valuable insight about inclusive and respectful language regarding gender variations. Jim Detmer encouraged me every step of the way to remain focused on my goals for writing this book. Eric Muhr provided truly insightful editing to a first-time author, and George Stevens translated a random list of likes and dislikes into a beautiful design for the book. Scott Beck made posing for the dreaded author's photo a very relaxing and enjoyable process.

Dozens of men have participated in my therapy group, Out Late, over the past ten years, and their honesty and resilience are woven throughout my writing. I deeply appreciate all they have taught me. I especially want to thank the writers of the "Dear Me" letters included in this book. I know their hard-earned wisdom will help many others.

On a personal level, I want to thank my former wife, Vickie, and our children, Maggie and Ben. We went through quite a journey as a family and as individuals. Their support in sharing some of our experiences means the world to me, and I love them all very much. Last but certainly not least, I thank my partner, Matt, whose love, support, and patience bless and fulfill my life every day. I am the luckiest! Thank you!

About the Author

William Brown hails from the town of Hays, Kansas, where he was raised with his three older sisters. He graduated from a private Catholic high school before attending Northwestern University as a theater major. He married shortly after graduation and began working as a professional actor in Chicago. Following the birth of his daughter, the family moved to Bloomington, Indiana, for his wife to pursue an MBA. Her career first took them to Fort Wayne, Indiana, where their son was born. William became primarily a stay-at-home dad and part-time actor. His wife's corporate career took them to Tennessee, Florida, Connecticut, Virginia, and finally to Atlanta, Georgia.

After coming out and the subsequent divorce, William attended Georgia State University for his Master's Degree in Clinical Mental Health Counseling. His coursework included a practicum and internship at Ridgeview Institute, a mental health hospital treating addiction and psychological issues. After graduating, he worked at The Equality Counseling Center with supervision from Becky Beaton, Ph.D., LPC. He started his private practice, William Brown Counseling Services, in 2015, and his focus includes working with the LGBTQ+ community on a cross-section of mental health issues. He established a therapy group called Out Late for those coming out later in life in 2012, and he works extensively with individuals and couples facing the reality of a spouse coming out as gay or bisexual. He partnered with several colleagues to establish The LGBTQ Therapist Resource, an association of affirming mental health providers that seeks to improve access to safe, competent therapists for LGBTQ+ identified individuals in Georgia.

Today, William lives with his partner, Matt, and their two sweet dogs, Annie and Iggy. They have four adult children between them, and they enjoy hopping on a plane to get away whenever they can—at least now that we can hop on planes again!

Glossary

advocacy: a task in sexual identity development where a person takes actions that support individual and group acceptance and rights for the LGBTQ+ community, which can be formal or informal in nature

affectional attraction: the desire and expression of physical and emotional intimacy and closeness outside of sex

AIDS: acquired immunodeficiency syndrome

agender: the absence of feeling a need to label or identify individual gender

anal sex: sex act involving anal penetration from one partner to another

analingus: oral stimulation of the anus using the mouth and tongue

armageddon factor: fear that coming out will utterly destroy a person's world and relationships

aromantic: the absence of feeling a need for romance and/or romantic attachments *bear:* a gay man whose physical presentation usually includes a beard, body hair, and a rounder shape

bisexual: an internal setting where a person finds themselves sexually and affectionately attracted to more than one gender

bottom: one who receives anal penetration in sex

bull: gay man with a bodybuilder physique

chlamydia: a bacterial sexually transmitted infection that can infect the genital, anal, or oral regions, which is treated with an antibiotic

cisgender: someone whose gender assigned at birth is in alignment with their gender identity

collaborative divorce: a type of divorce process where the parties agree to keep the proceedings out of a court of law and under the jurisdiction of a mediator, often in an effort to lower financial and emotional costs

coming out: the process of disclosing one's identity as something other than straight or cisgender through word or action

consensual nonmonogamy: an agreement between relationship partners to have the freedom to pursue or experience sexual activities outside of the relationship itself

conversion therapy: various therapeutic interventions that were developed to try to return a person to heterosexuality and binary gender identification

cub: a younger gay male who will often have a beard and body hair and have physical characteristics similar to a bear

daddy: an older gay male

denial: a psychological state that leaves a person unable to name or see an uncomfortable truth

DILF: "daddy I'd like to fuck"—an attractive older male

faulty beliefs: falsehoods based on myth, stereotypes, or direct lies that support a person's denial about their sexual identity

fidelity: sexual boundaries agreed to within a relationship, which may include anything from monogamy or consensual nonmonogamy

gay: an internal setting that finds the same gender primarily, but not necessarily exclusively, sexually and affectionately attractive, most commonly speaking of men (non-women) attracted to men (non-women)

gender: a range of identity-based characteristics pertaining to masculinity and femininity

gender expression: ways in which a person expresses gender through historically socially normed identifiers in appearance and physical attributes, such as a dress for a woman or a suit and tie for a man

gold star gay: a gay man who has never had sexual contact with a vagina

gonorrhea: a bacterial sexually transmitted infection that can infect genitals, the anus and rectum, mouth and throat, or the eyes, which is treated with antibiotics

herpes: a viral sexually transmitted infection that may infect the genital, anus and rectum, or lips, mouth, and throat, whose symptoms may be managed with medication but cannot be cured

heteronormative: tied to the socially understood customs in behavior and relationship between heterosexuals

HIV: human immunodeficiency virus that can be easily transmitted through anal sex without using a condom. HIV can be managed with medications but that, if left untreated, could progress to AIDS

homophobia: the irrational fear of, aversion to, or discrimination against homosexuality or homosexuals

HPV: human papillomavirus infection, which is a viral infection that can be sexually transmitted and sometimes results in warts and possible testicular impacts

identity development: a theoretical description of the steps a person moves through as they come to know and understand specific aspects of self, such as sexual identity

immersion: a task in sexual identity development when a person places themselves into settings where the assumption in that setting is that most people present are gay

internalized homophobia: feelings of shame, guilt, anger, and disgust for one's own homosexuality

intersex: when genitalia are not specifically identifiable as a penis or vagina

jock: a gay man who is muscular and athletic in physique and perhaps enjoys playing sports

lesbian: a woman (non-man) who is primarily, but not necessarily exclusively, attracted to other women (non-men)

marginalization: actions and words that reinforce and maintain a lower status due to minority designations such as race, sexuality, or gender

mixed-orientation marriage: a marriage where the two partners do not share the same sexual identity

monkeypox: a viral infection that can be spread from person to person through close skin contact, often resulting in flu-like symptoms followed by a rash with painful blisters *monogamy:* one form of fidelity where two people agree to only engage in sexual activity with each other

nonbinary: gender identification that is neither exclusively male nor female

open relationship: a primary relationship where the members mutually establish and practice a defined consensual nonmonogamy

otter: a gay man who is thin, with lots of body hair and a beard

pansexual: no specific preference for sexual or gender identity in sexual and affectional attraction

platinum gay: a gay man who has never had sexual contact with a vagina and was also born through c-section

polyamorous: a romantic relationship structure that involves more than two people

poppers: chemicals from the alkyl nitrate family, most commonly amyl, which are commonly used in sex between men. They provide a rush of feeling horny, and they relax stiff muscles in the anus and sphincter

PrEP: pre-exposure prophylaxis, medication that is taken daily to help prevent an HIV infection

PEP: post-exposure prophylaxis, medication that is started within forty-eight hours of exposure to HIV that can help prevent infection

PTSD: post-traumatic stress disorder, a clinical diagnosis with common symptoms of hypervigilance, fear, panic, etc., related to experiencing or witnessing either a single or multiple traumatic events

queer: an inclusive umbrella term that includes all variations of non-straight and non-cisgender identities

questioning: when an individual is unsure of what labels or identities, if any, apply to their sexuality and gender

religious trauma: a result of shame and sometimes direct emotional or physical harm from religious teachings and practices that identify a person's sexual or gender identity as sinful and damnable

rimming: a common descriptor for oral stimulation of the anus using the lips, mouth, or tongue, also sometimes referred to as "tossing the salad"

second adolescence: the return of feelings and behaviors related to teenage adolescence after coming out later in life

sexual identity: a person's internal setting that indicates who and what they find sexually and affectionately attractive

sexual orientation: a synonym for sexual identity that indicates who and what a person finds sexually and affectionately attractive

side: a preference for some gay men to have sex without anal sex in any form

straight: sexual and affectional attraction to a different gender almost exclusively, specifically men attracted to women and women attracted to men

syphilis: a bacterial sexually transmitted infection that may infect the genitals, anal area, mouth, or eyes and will sometimes initially cause visible sores. This infection can progress to further stages that may lead to significant health issues or death if untreated. It can be cured with antibiotic treatment.

top: a person who penetrates another person in sexual activity, whether orally, anally, or vaginally

transgender: gender identity that does not match the gender assigned at birth

twink: a young, thin, and more hairless gay man

twunk: a young, muscular, and more hairless gay man

versatile: someone who enjoys the top and bottom positions in sexual activity

wolf: a bear type who prefers to remain single

References

Introduction

Higgins, D. Gay. "Men from Heterosexual Marriages: Attitudes, Behaviors, Childhood Experiences, and Reasons for Marriage," *Journal of Homosexuality*, Vol 42(4) 2002.

Hernandez, B., Schwenke, N., and Colwick, M. "Spouses in Mixed-Orientation Marriage: A 20-Year Review of Empirical Studies," *Journal of Marital and Family Therapy*, Vol 37(3) 2011.

"Acronyms Explained," outrightinternational.org, Published September 20, 2021.

Chapter 2

Morton, M., Dworsky, A., and Samuels, G. "Missed Opportunities: Youth Homelessness in America: National Estimates," Chapin Hall at University of Chicago, 2017.

Chapter 4

Dube, S., Anda, R., Whitfield, C., *et al.* "Long-term Consequences of Childhood Sexual Abuse by Gender of Victim," *American Journal of Preventive Medicine*, Vol 28 2005.

Briere, J. & Elliot, D. "Prevalence and Psychological Sequelae of Self-Reported Childhood Physical and Sexual Abuse in a General Population Sample of Men and Women." *Child Abuse & Neglect*, Vol 27 2003.

Holmes, W. & Slap, G. "Sexual Abuse of Boys: Definition, Prevalence, Correlates, Sequelae, and Management," *Journal of the American Medical Association* (JAMA), Vol 280 1998.

Lisak, D., Hopper, J. & Song, P. "Factors in the Cycle of Violence: Gender Rigidity and Emotional Constriction," *Journal of Traumatic Stress*, Vol 9 1996.

Finkelhor, D., Hotaling, G., Lewis, I., & Smith, C. "Sexual Abuse in a National Survey of Adult Men and Women: Prevalence, Characteristics, and Risk Factors," *Child Abuse & Neglect*, Vol 14 1990.

Holmes, G., Offen, L., & Waller, G. "See No Evil, Hear No Evil, Speak No Evil: Why Do Relatively Few Male Victims of Childhood Sexual Abuse Receive Help for Abuse-Related Issues in Adulthood?" *Clinical Psychology Review*, Vol 17 1997.

Chapter 6

Lyons, B. *et al.* "Suicides Among Lesbian and Gay Male Individuals: Findings from the National Violent Death Reporting System," *American Journal of Preventative Medicine*, Vol 56 (4).

Chapter 8

"A Workplace Divided: Understanding the Climate for LGBTQ Workers Nationwide," Human Rights Campaign, 2018.

Chapter 10

Kelly, J. Risk and *Protective Factors Associated with Child and Adolescent Adjustment Following Separation and Divorce, Parenting Plan Evaluations: Applied Research for the Family Court*, Oxford University Press, 2012.

Chapter 13

Cass, V. "Homosexual Identity Formation: A Theoretical Model," *Journal of Homosexuality* Vol 4(3), 1979.

Kaufman, J. and Johnson, C. "Stigmatized Individuals and the Process of Identity," *The Sociology Quarterly*, Vol 45(4), 2004.

Chapter 17

Stag, P. "Do's and Don't's of Poppers," Alphatribe, 2021.

Chapter 18

"HIV Basics—Statistics," Center for Disease Control and Prevention, 2019.

"HIV Basics—Overview, Data, and Trends," hiv.org, 2020.

"CDC Fact Sheet: What Gay, Bisexual and Other Men Who Have Sex with Men Need to Know About Sexually Transmitted Diseases," Center for Disease Control and Prevention, 2022.

"Gonorrhea—CDC Fact Sheet," Center for Disease Control and Prevention, 2022.

"Chlamydia—CDC Fact Sheet," Center for Disease Control and Prevention, 2022.

"Syphilis & MSM (Men Who Have Sex with Men)—CDC Fact Sheet," Center for Disease Control and Prevention, 2022.

"Genital Herpes—CDC Fact Sheet," Center for Disease Control and Prevention, 2022.

"HPV and Men—CDC Fact Sheet," Center for Disease Control and Prevention, 2022.

"Monkeypox—CDC Fact Sheet," Center for Disease Control and Prevention, 2022.

Chapter 19

"2018 National Survey on Drug Use and Health: Lesbian, Gay, Bisexual (LGB) Adults (Annual Report)," Substance Abuse and Mental Health Services Administration (SAMHSA), Published January 14, 2020.

Chapter 22

Smith, E. "From Stonewall to Pride 50: The History of the Pride Parade," Refinery29.com, June 6, 2019.

www.ingramcontent.com/pod-product-compliance
Lightning Source LLC
Chambersburg PA
CBHW022049020426
42335CB00012B/608